Archaeology

A Beginner's Guide

T0109256

ONEWORLD BEGINNER'S GUIDES combine an original, inventive, and engaging approach with expert analysis. Innovative and affordable, books in the series are perfect for anyone curious about the way the world works and the big ideas of our time.

aesthetics
africa
american politics
anarchism
animal behaviour
anthropology
anti-capitalism
aquinas
art
artificial intelligence
the baha'i faith
the beat generation
the bible
biodiversity
bioterror & biowarfare
the brain
british politics
the Buddha
cancer
censorship
christianity
civil liberties
classical music
climate change
cloning
the cold war
conservation
crimes against humanity
criminal psychology
critical thinking
the crusades
daoism
democracy
descartes
dewey
dyslexia

energy
engineering
the english civil wars
the enlightenment
epistemology
ethics
the european union
evolution
evolutionary psychology
existentialism
fair trade
feminism
forensic science
french literature
the french revolution
genetics
global terrorism
hinduism
the history of medicine
history of science
homer
humanism
huxley
iran
islamic philosophy
the islamic veil
journalism
judaism
lacan
life in the universe
literary theory
machiavelli
mafia & organized crime
magic
marx
medieval philosophy

the middle east
modern slavery
NATO
the new testament
nietzsche
nineteenth-century art
the northern ireland conflict
nutrition
oil
opera
the palestine–israeli conflict
particle physics
paul
philosophy
philosophy of mind
philosophy of religion
philosophy of science
planet earth
postmodernism
psychology
quantum physics
the qur'an
racism
reductionism
religion
renaissance art
the roman empire
the russian revolution
shakespeare
the small arms trade
sufism
the torah
the united nations
volcanoes
world war II

Archaeology

A Beginner's Guide

Joe Flatman

ONEWORLD

A Oneworld Paperback Original

First published by Oneworld Publications, 2015

ISBN 978-1-78074-503-9
eBook ISBN 978-1-78074-504-6

Typeset by Siliconchips Services Ltd, UK
Printed and bound in Great Britain
by Clays Ltd, St Ives plc

Oneworld Publications
10 Bloomsbury Street
London WC1B 3SR
England

To Zoe from Daddy, autumn 2014

Contents

List of illustrations viii

1 What is (and isn't) archaeology? 1

2 Tools and techniques 22

3 The archaeology of objects 62

4 The archaeology of places 90

5 The archaeology of landscapes 127

6 The archaeology of travelling 147

7 The future of archaeology 163

Further reading 168

Acknowledgements 181

Index 182

List of illustrations

Figure 1 Harris matrix stratigraphic sequence diagram from the medieval Wild's Rents tannery

Figure 2 C14 probability distributions of dates from Brisley Farm, Ashford, Kent

Figure 3 Excavations under way in advance of a city-centre redevelopment at Eastgate Square, Chichester

Figure 4 Archaeologists at work in the historic Rocks district of Sydney

Figure 5 Fountains Abbey, North Yorkshire, founded in 1132 CE; Britain's largest monastic ruin and most complete Cistercian abbey

Figure 6 Prehistoric footprint impression surviving in the intertidal mud of the Severn Estuary in south-west Britain

Figure 7 The Iron Bridge and village of Ironbridge in Shropshire, the birthplace of the global Industrial Revolution

Figure 8 Mile castle 39 (also known as Castle Nick), a Roman fortification along Hadrian's Wall, occupied until the late fourth century CE

Figure 9 Kenilworth Castle, Warwickshire

Figure 10 The ship is the most common figurative motif in Scandinavian rock art

Figure 11   Replica of a thirteenth-century CE model boat found in the Viking city of Dublin

Figure 12   Reconstruction of the use of the thirteenth-century CE model boat found in Dublin

Figure 13   Archaeologists at work on the wreck of the steamboat *Montana*, near Bridgeton, Missouri

1
What is (and isn't) archaeology?

In the popular imagination, archaeology is either about travel, adventure and intrigue or about people with marginal dress sense droning on about dusty old bits of pot. The reality lies somewhere in between: most archaeologists can tell you real stories of adventure in a foreign land; all can equally tell of days, weeks or months of painstaking work in a dusty archive or library. Most archaeologists don't stand out in a crowd and live a life much like any other person, driving to the office and spending too long on a computer dealing with emails before calling at the supermarket to pick up some food on the way home. They have families and pets and personal lives; in the evening they watch box sets of DVDs on their television, eat pizza and worry about cleaning the kitchen.

What makes archaeologists different is not normally the nature of their daily lives but rather how they view the world, in particular how they approach and interpret physical remains, both of the present and the past. Having an archaeological training is like having a special pair of glasses that transforms your view of the world: once worn, nothing ever quite looks the same again. From the smallest piece of pottery to a giant building, ship or landscape, approaching the world with an archaeological mindset means having a fundamentally different view of everything, because it involves seeing the present through the lens of all the

activities and processes that have gone before. When an archaeologist walks down the street they visualise the layers of previous
occupation underlying the modern asphalt and concrete; layers
going back perhaps hundreds or thousands of years. When they
walk into a building they visualise the buildings that came before
that lie buried beneath the modern bricks and mortar; when they
sit on the seashore they wonder about the people who hunted
and fished along that same shore perhaps tens of thousands of
years ago, and when they light a match, cook some food or hold
a pen, they think about the countless industrial and intellectual
processes that led up to them being able to perform those simple
actions. They think about how people a hundred, a thousand or
ten thousand years ago would have created fire, found and cooked
food or made their mark on the world. Moreover, these archaeologists know how to uncover the physical remains of these past
streets, buildings, beaches and objects and how to securely identify, date and protect them for future generations.

This book is more about how to *think* like an archaeologist
than it is about how to *be* an archaeologist. It uses examples – of
places, landscapes, objects and peoples – from the past and the
present to demonstrate how archaeologists approach the world.
It explains how archaeologists weigh up the pros and cons of
different types of evidence, how they formulate and test hypotheses and how they come to new conclusions about life in the
past. And, although focused on archaeological sites, it also uses
documentary evidence such as historical texts and photographs,
together with artistic evidence such as ancient drawings and
carvings, and ethnographic and anthropological evidence such as
oral history, photography and interview records, because a good
archaeologist is open to all available sources of evidence.

As the doyen of British archaeology Mortimer Wheeler
(1890–1976) wrote in his 1954 book *Archaeology from the Earth*:
'the archaeologist is digging up not things but people.' As true
now as it was then, being an archaeologist means many things

but it is certainly never boring, because humans are complex and fascinating creatures, as were the worlds that they built in the past.

Practising archaeology

Put simply, archaeology is the study of past human societies through the analysis of surviving physical remains. It is both a practical and theoretical pursuit. Archaeology's practical focus lies in the development and application of tools and techniques for maximising the search for, and analysis and conservation of, physical remains. But this practical focus does not alone make 'archaeology'. Anyone can search for and recover ancient objects but that is treasure-hunting, not archaeology. What makes it archaeology is the combination of practical endeavour and a theoretical focus. Archaeology means attempting to understand the past, to interpret what the physical remains discovered tell us about how our common ancestors lived, what motivations underlay the making of these objects and how they influenced their landscapes. Archaeologists take pains to communicate this past to non-archaeologists and to involve them in the exploration, discovery, interpretation and protection of historic sites. Any projects that do not involve all of these different processes are not archaeology.

Archaeology has a long tradition of working closely with other disciplines and, indeed, has its roots in a mixture of antiquarianism, geology and classical studies. But these foundation stones of archaeology are only part of its story. As archaeology has become more of a scientific process, close ties have been established with the many different branches of science. All the sciences have practical and theoretical approaches that archaeologists have adapted to use in their study of ancient materials, places and peoples. And since the majority of actual physical archaeology undertaken these days is the result of work in advance of the building of new houses, industry, energy and transport facilities, this means that subjects such as geography and planning share many practical and theoretical approaches with archaeology; the practical being *how* work is done and the theoretical *why* – why people choose to live in or develop a specific place and what that means for their physical environment.

Archaeology is different from related disciplines such as anthropology and social geography in that it is primarily focused on the physical remains of ancient societies and the study of what these remains can tell us about past peoples. Anthropologists are just as interested in people as archaeologists but they use different tools and techniques (such as interviews, sound and image recordings and long-term observation undertaken while living and working among the communities that they study) and are concerned with the study of living communities. Similarly, geographers are also interested in people and how they influence physical places but their work differs from archaeologists in its scale: most geographers are concerned with people on a much larger scale – as communities and populations – and the focus of their analyses lies away from the people and their immediate physical traces that fascinate archaeologists.

Archaeologists use similar approaches to these disciplines but take a different path. Using a variety of tools and techniques, archaeologists focus on the minutiae of the physical traces of the past to find out about communities, groups and ultimately individuals. There are some specific practices that are essential to archaeology and more or less define it. These include:

- *Physical remains:* a focus on exploring the physical remains of ancient societies and the interpretation of these remains using scientific analyses.
- *Scientific approaches:* a commitment to advancing practical, especially scientifically repeatable, methods of identifying, exploring and analysing the past.

- *Dating:* paying considerable attention to the chronology of different cultures' relative development and, within this, a focus on the accurate, 'absolute' dating of materials, processes and activities through scientific means.
- *Context:* an emphasis on the importance of 'context' – the relative position of the different materials and features of an archaeological site that indicate the processes of the site's formation, particularly its *stratigraphy*; that is, the relationship of materials and features to those above and below.
- *Integrity:* in the light of all of these points, an emphasis on maintaining the overall integrity of a site if at all possible, keeping destructive excavation as the last option and preferring to preserve sites *in situ* (in place). This includes a commitment to 'preservation by record' of sites and materials where these have of necessity been excavated. This last point includes a commitment to public engagement and communal ethics in archaeology, to acting responsibly and sharing approaches, data and results for the common benefit of humankind.

Summing up this range of practical, theoretical and ethical concerns, archaeology can thus be defined as the study of the surviving physical remains of ancient societies and the appreciation – and communication – of the relevance of these ancient materials to the contemporary world and its present and future societies.

Ethics

The balance of practice and theory in archaeology includes a well-defined ethical stance. Just as doctors and lawyers have ethical codes, so do archaeologists. Archaeologists' ethical codes focus on the responsible collection of evidence in a manner that respects the views and beliefs of ancient and modern communities.

Archaeologists do not act in a high-handed manner; they strive to minimise damage to ancient sites and materials (that is, they do not recover materials for sale and only excavate sites when strictly necessary) and they promote the concept of the common ownership of ancient materials by all humankind and the need to provide access to these materials and the information derived from their study (that is, share information about the past with as many people as possible). This last point has been known to come into conflict with the first; not all Indigenous communities, for example, are happy for their cultures to be studied by archaeologists in this manner.

THE CONTROL OF THE PAST

Archaeologists' belief in the common ownership of the past by humankind is nowhere more strongly contested than in the case of Indigenous communities' control of cultural materials.

Archaeologists argue for the need to share access to and information about the past in line with generally accepted scientific methods, including peer review and repeatable experiments. The argument goes that work undertaken ought to include verifiable data that can be analysed independently, and thus archaeological sites and materials ought to be similarly accessible. But this perspective is based in a Western scientific tradition that is sometimes at odds with Indigenous communities' views about the interpretation of, access to, and ultimately control of historic materials.

Many Indigenous communities dispute such approaches to the past. Their cultures often emphasise a more controlled and respectful relationship with ancestral materials than is common among communities of European origin. Within this, many Indigenous communities dispute chronological frameworks of 'past', 'present' and 'future'; to them, their ancestors are often part of the present, and under such circumstances, elders and other key individuals negotiate the broader cultural relationship with and engagement between present-day communities and ancestral peoples, sites and materials. In this negotiation, access to specific types of information, material and even places is dependent on the age, gender or social status of individuals, as well as the time of year and ritual context of engagement. Such an approach often puts such communities at odds with both the general population of an area and with scientific communities such as archaeologists.

Confrontation over the ownership of the past has its roots in the abuse of Indigenous communities by European colonisers in the Americas, Africa and Australasia from the fifteenth century onwards. Descendent Indigenous communities, many of which were driven to the brink of extinction by European settlers, began to fight back against this oppression in the 1960s and 1970s, as part of the wider civil rights movement. Part of this movement included the legal reclamation of ancestral lands, as well as cultural materials and even human remains, many thousands of examples of which had been held for study in museums since the nineteenth and early twentieth centuries.

In the USA, the most important law in relation to this issue is the Native American Graves Protection and Repatriation Act (NAGPRA) of 1990. NAGPRA is a law that requires federal agencies and institutions that receive federal funding to return Native American cultural items to their respective peoples. NAGPRA established a programme of federal grants to assist in this repatriation, up to and including the enforcement of civil penalties on museums that failed to comply with returning such materials. NAGPRA states that Native American remains belong to lineal descendants. If lineal descendants cannot be identified, then the remains belong either to the tribe on whose lands they were found or to the tribes with the closest known relationship. A criminal provision of the Act prohibits trafficking in Native American human remains or cultural items.

Many communities complain that the legal processes of NAGPRA bias the system against them. This is because the burden of proof in NAGPRA requires communities to demonstrate a relationship that may not be well documented or understood, or in which privileged information relating to cultural materials or ancestral knowledge has to be disclosed. None the less, the remains of about 32,000 individuals have been returned to their respective tribes since the Act came into force, together with hundreds of thousands of related cultural materials.

Popular perceptions of archaeology

Archaeology, both real and imaginary, is a staple of popular culture. Turn on a television almost anywhere in the world at almost any time of day and you're likely to find a programme involving archaeology, from a 1930s film to a cutting-edge documentary, or reruns of films such as the *Indiana Jones* or *Lara Croft* series. Meanwhile, long-running television series such as *Time Team* have made archaeology a familiar part of everyday life. When you can buy a toy model or a computer game based on the exploits of a fictional archaeologist, you know that the subject is definitely a part of mainstream culture.

In private, archaeologists might bemoan many of the public representations of both archaeologists and archaeology but few are overly worried by them. Clichés abound for almost every job in the world, from archaeology, to police work, to the law or medicine, to name just four. But there is one minority area of 'pop archaeology' that needs to be addressed: 'pseudo-archaeology'. This fringe, with its often vociferous members, does genuine harm to archaeology, and especially to archaeological sites. A small but influential community is involved in actual physical activity on archaeological sites that is, in varying degrees, damaging, destructive and frankly disastrous. Some of this is state sanctioned, such as the Taliban's destruction in 2001, on religious grounds, of the two statues of Buddha carved into the cliffs at Bamiyan in Afghanistan. But much of this destruction is the consequence of private enterprise, driven by the pursuit of short-term financial profit: looting and treasure-hunting. At one end of the scale are lone individuals or small groups looting single sites or small areas. At the opposite end of the scale is well-financed and formal looting by commercial organisations. Often working under the guise of what they term legitimate salvage – increasingly rephrased as 'commercial archaeology' – these organisations feed the international trade in antiquities. But such work simply *isn't* archaeology.

Archaeological fieldwork can involve going to exotic or remote places and even undertaking mildly dangerous activities, such as diving underwater or abseiling down a cliff, but this is not the driving force of archaeology. An archaeologist is an archaeologist because he or she seeks to find out more about the human past and share that information. Archaeologists are adaptable, going to different places and using different tools and techniques to help answer their questions and test their hypotheses about the past. Sometimes that means going somewhere and doing something adventurous but most of the time it means going to or working in very safe and mundane environments.

Most importantly, archaeology isn't about treasure-hunting. If the primary goal, or even a major component, of any project is the recovery of historic materials for sale and profit, this is not archaeology. This is not to say that archaeology cannot make money: professional archaeologists earn their living in all sorts of ways, such as teaching archaeology in schools and universities, managing archaeological sites on behalf of either private owners or governments, or carefully excavating in advance of new developments. Nor is it to say that materials cannot be recovered; only that there must be a valid reason for the recovery, accompanied by careful recording, conservation, eventual display in a museum or archive and ensuring it is accessible to future scholars. But no reputable professional archaeologist makes money from recovering and selling artefacts. Indeed, to do so puts him or her at odds with every existing professional code of conduct and ethics for archaeologists. When archaeologists go into the field they have a professional duty to do their best work, to damage archaeological sites as little as possible, to recover objects only if absolutely necessary, to conserve recovered materials for public engagement and future analysis, and to publish the results of their work in a timely manner. This means that archaeologists actively seek to discourage and combat the illicit trade in antiquities, and to know and comply with all the laws applicable to their professional activities. It also means that archaeologists will always work to preserve the scientific integrity of sites, to conserve archaeological sites and materials as a resource for study and enjoyment now and in the future, and to encourage others to do the same.

A brief history of archaeology

Archaeology's roots go back to the antiquarians of the seventeenth and eighteenth centuries. Antiquarian archaeology involved a tiny group of people, all white, middle or upper class, and almost all men, working on the surviving evidence of past cultures. This included work both on excavated physical remains and also on historical documents in the major European industrialised nations and the USA. One of the first people in North America to practise what we now call 'archaeology' was Thomas Jefferson (1743–1826), third President of the United States, although he would not have referred to himself as an archaeologist but as an antiquarian: a student of antiquities. Such individuals did much good work but also much that was bad. The best were instrumental in the formalisation of the study of the material remains of the past; the worst were nothing better than looters and charlatans who enjoyed 'excavating' – the modern term would be pillaging – historic sites for the pleasure of destruction and the recovery of precious materials such as ancient jewellery.

Slowly, through the work of good practitioners, and under the auspices of the organisations they set up, such as the Society of Antiquaries of London (founded in 1707 and still active), the archaeological study of the past became an informal scholarly process within a social network. Although antiquarians were not archaeologists in the modern definition of the term, they set in place the foundations for the later practical and theoretical development of the discipline. Such individuals also helped to make antiquarian endeavour acceptable, raising its profile and status and paving the way for its formal scientific development and eventual place in schools, universities and government.

By the later nineteenth century, the work of antiquarians had begun to expand beyond the horizons of earlier scholars. However, these scholars, although they thought along the lines of modern archaeology, were generally unsystematic in their studies, approaches and interests. The change that came about was in part due to a greater emphasis on formal scientific enquiry and recording that emerged in the later nineteenth century. This was when the term 'archaeology' (from the modern Latin *archaeologia*, derived from the Greek *arkhaiologia* 'ancient history' and *arkhaios* 'ancient') first appeared in its modern form.

The expanding world of the sciences, especially the natural sciences such as geology (in which many archaeologists of the nineteenth century were experienced), had a great impact on the formal study of antiquity, particularly the burgeoning study of prehistory. Two examples are the work of the geologist Charles Lyell (1797–1875) on the geological antiquity and form of the earth, and the naturalist Charles Darwin (1809–1882) on the principles of evolution and natural selection. A key contemporary, albeit much less well known outside archaeology, was Christian Jürgensen Thomsen (1788–1865), a Danish archaeologist who developed the chronological three-age system of prehistoric time periods, named after their respective tool-making technologies: the Stone Age (approximately 3.4 million years BCE to 4500–2000 BCE), Bronze Age (approximately 3600 BCE to 600–300 BCE) and Iron Age (approximately 1300 BCE to 600–200 BCE). Thomsen's analyses formed the basis of the chronologies of archaeology used across Europe to this day.

Through the influence of such people, the chronology of the antiquity of the earth and of humanity began to be properly understood. In turn, archaeology as a discipline began to be formalised as a social science. This formalisation included absorbing science's lessons of rigorous and consistent record-keeping and experiment.

At the same time that people such as Lyell, Darwin and Thomsen were proving the antiquity and evolutionary origins of the human race, the existing practices of earlier antiquarians began to be integrated into a system of archaeological survey, excavation and post-excavation analysis. Researchers such as Augustus Lane-Fox Pitt Rivers (1827–1900), working in the UK, and William Flinders Petrie (1853–1942), working in Egypt, developed systematic processes to ensure that when archaeological sites were destroyed by excavation, as full a documentary record as possible would be made. Pitt Rivers, often referred to as the 'father of British archaeology', is credited with developing the first system-atic approach to archaeological excavation, in which the context and significance of all materials and features discovered are taken into consideration and careful records are made of the process of excavation. Flinders Petrie, in contrast, was a pioneer of the systematic recording and study of artefacts and the first to use 'seri-ation' (creating a pattern of dates for objects by placing materials, such as pottery, in stylistic order) to establish the basic chronology of a site. Pitt Rivers, Flinders Petrie and others established the key archaeological principle of 'preservation by record'; that is, if you destroy a site through excavation you must leave as accurate a written record of your work and discoveries as possible for future generations to analyse. In the process, such individuals also began to clarify two key considerations of the practice of archaeology: first, the need to place excavation within a social matrix of under-standing, both of other sites within a physical landscape and also within an analytical framework (for example, the concept of the systematic research of the past) and second, the need to system-atically map and record the locations of all sites in order both to analyse their potential for formal investigation and, crucially, to protect them for future generations. This was the beginning of the legal protection of archaeological sites, something that Pitt Rivers was instrumental in pursuing in the development and passing of the Ancient Monuments Protection Act (1882). This was the first such legislation in Britain; similar legislation was enacted at this time around the world to protect historic sites.

In the 1920s and 1930s, as much of the world recovered from the ravages of the First World War, archaeology became increasingly diverse. At one level were archaeologists working on similar sites and using similar techniques to the founding fathers such as Pitt Rivers. The Australian archaeologist Vere Gordon Childe (1892–1957) did much excellent, but often undervalued, field-work exploring the prehistoric civilisations of Europe. Childe was the first person to fully synthesise archaeological data from a variety of sources to develop a comprehensive understanding of the form and process of prehistory, formalising for the first time the basic understanding of these periods that remains in use, albeit with modifications. Work was also under way in the Americas, undertaken by archaeologists such as Alfred Kidder (1885–1963), whose application of archaeological techniques to prehistory in this region was instrumental in the formal develop-ment of scientific approaches in North American archaeology. However, only limited professional training in the practice of archaeology was available, something that soon began to change. The British archaeologists Mortimer Wheeler and his first wife, Tessa Verney Wheeler (1893–1936), were emblematic of this type of archaeologist, as well as being instrumental in reform-ing the system, spending their lives expanding both the practi-cal tools and techniques of archaeologists. The Wheelers helped to dramatically improve the quality of archaeological fieldwork and training around the world. A well-known colleague of the Wheelers was Kathleen Kenyon (1906–1978), probably the most famous British female archaeologist. Her work on Neolithic sites in the Middle East (especially at Jericho) transformed our under-standing of those civilisations, as well as being a key training loca-tion in excavation techniques and ceramic classification methods for many future archaeologists.

Further afield, an increasingly influential body of individuals was at work in scattered schools located adjacent to the archaeo-logical sites that many people were increasingly interested in exca-vating, especially in the Near and Middle East and in major urban centres such as Rome, Athens, Jerusalem and Baghdad. These people were often associated with European colonial control; few were paid archaeologists and most had private incomes. Around them circulated a far larger band of semi-professional archaeologists of very mixed background and ability. This period is considered a golden age of archaeology, enjoyed by a chosen few. It is the world of archaeology depicted by the novelist Agatha Christie (1890–1976) in her books *Death on the Nile* and *Murder in Mesopotamia*; her second husband, Max Mallowan (1904–1978), was one of those semi-professional archaeologists. It is also the world that inspires many modern depictions of archaeology, from the *Indiana Jones* and *Mummy* film series to the *Lara Croft* video games and films. Thanks to the efforts of these different groups of archaeologists, by the start of the Second World War the discipline of archaeology was tentatively established around the world, based in university and museum systems and, if not thriving, then at least existing with a clear identity, structure and community.

NAZI IDEOLOGY AND ARCHAEOLOGY

The twenty-first century has seen a resurgence of archaeologically justified racial mythmaking. Far-right groups continually perpetrate a myth of 'Aryan' superiority that is based on a misunderstanding of archaeological data – in particular, on a misunderstanding of the phasing of different communities and their genetic 'purity' – that is simply wrong. Such groups misappropriate evidence of Anglo-Saxon communities in Europe in their search for an imagined and strongly nationalistic, Aryan-centric national prehistory. Archaeology has shown such communities to have been far more mixed, both culturally and genetically, than was previously believed. These were not racially 'pure' communities living an isolated and culturally homogenous life but rather a far more fascinating mélange of peoples, cultures and materials, with wide international trade links and extensive interbreeding, as shown by the extent of 'Viking' communities' physical and genetic remains, which are scattered across modern-day Scandinavia, Europe and western Asia, well beyond their traditionally perceived boundaries.

Nazi archaeology originated in the movement, led by various Nazi leaders in the 1930s, to research the German past in order to strengthen German nationalism. This movement, which set out to bring a mythical version of the Roman Empire back to Germany, was based on the ideas of Tacitus's *Germania*, written about 98 CE. This obsession fed into wider Nazi myths and mysticism and was a central part of the cultural identity of the Nazis, especially in their use of symbols such as runes (a Germanic and Scandinavian alphabet) in their military insignia. Encouraged by Heinrich Himmler, from 1935 the *Ahnenerbe* (a Nazi think-tank organisation) sponsored research into the anthropological and cultural history of the Aryan race. The *Ahnenerbe* was particularly interested in promoting research that could be used to prove that prehistoric and mythological Nordic populations had once ruled the world. Fieldwork locations included numerous sites across Germany (and, after the invasion of 1939, in annexed Poland), the Karelia region of Finland, the Bohuslän region of south-western Sweden, the Val Camonica region of Italy, and various locations in the Middle East, including modern-day Turkey, Greece, Syria and Iraq. In 1937, Nazi scholars even travelled as far afield as Tibet, in an attempt to prove that early Aryans had conquered much of Asia. Such explorations have entered the modern popular imagination through films such as the *Indiana Jones* and *Hellboy* franchises, both of which include reference to the work of the *Ahnenerbe*.

Archaeology after the Second World War was influenced by a series of interrelated developments. The damage that the war inflicted on many cities and landscapes had one sort of impact. The need to rebuild major cities, such as London, led to many archaeological sites being discovered and studied. Alongside this came the realisation that there were very few legal structures to protect archaeological sites or require them to be investigated before they were destroyed to make way for new developments. Large-scale urban planning, from the 1950s onwards, exacerbated this problem. Some major losses of archaeological sites and historic buildings of international importance occurred at this time, due to the unthinking implementation of new urban plans that gave no consideration to heritage.

The eventual outcome was the birth of the 'rescue' or 'salvage' archaeology movement, and archaeological organisations (often charities) dedicated to lobbying for the better protection of archaeological sites and undertaking emergency excavations on sites faced by destruction. The work of such organisations, most famously RESCUE (the British Trust for Archaeology), in time led to more extensive laws to protect archaeological sites, put in place in the 1980s and 1990s. This story is outlined in the 1973 book *Rescue Archaeology*, written by one of the leading rescue archaeologists of this era, Philip Rahtz (1921–2011).

Alongside the influence of rescue archaeology, more traditional forms of academic archaeology grew after the Second World War but for very different reasons. Expanded social mobility and the breakdown of traditional class barriers to higher education saw, from the 1950s, major growth in the university sectors in Europe, the USA, Australia and elsewhere. Archaeology flourished in this refreshed academic environment, with new departments springing up around the world. An example of the type of activities undertaken in this period can be gained from the work of Grahame Clark (1907–1995), a British archaeologist notable for his work on the Mesolithic and his theories on palaeoeconomy. His work moved archaeology away from its traditional preoccupation with stone-tool typologies towards a broader understanding of how early societies exploited their environments. A very different environment and approach was developed at around the same time by George Bass (1932–), an American archaeologist dubbed the 'father of underwater archaeology' for his groundbreaking work at a series of sites along the southern coast of Turkey from 1960 onwards. Bass's determination to undertake work underwater that was as methodologically consistent as work on land proved the significance of underwater archaeology in the study of ancient civilisations. Meanwhile, the type of archaeology being undertaken in such locations also changed. Linked to the reform of civil liberties and the gradual withdrawal of various European nations from formal colonisation, archaeology began to readdress its global scope and introverted cultural outlook. As I will discuss in Chapter 2, the radiocarbon revolution (the development of accurate types of scientific dating) aided this process, forcing a reconsideration of the antiquity of the human race and challenging preconceptions about relative levels of social development among different cultures and communities.

By the 1970s, alongside these new scientific techniques came new theoretical approaches to the human past, particularly influenced by the sciences, in what became known as the 'processual' school of archaeological thought. This approach to the past emphasises the need for analytical models of human behaviour to accompany the scientific analyses of individual materials. Based broadly on the principle of cultural evolution, processual archaeological theory argues that it is possible to understand past cultural systems through the systematic analysis of the remains of past societies. By applying scientific models to the past, processual theory suggests that culture can be defined as the result of exosomatic (outside the body) environmental adaptations by humans. Processual archaeologists argue that cultural change happens within a predictable framework and they seek to understand this framework by the analysis of its components. Moreover, since this framework is predictable, they argue that science is the key to unlocking how those components interacted with the cultural whole. Colin Renfrew (1937–) was and remains a leader in such approaches. A polymathic British archaeologist, Renfrew has, probably more than any other single person, helped to shape the modern discipline of archaeology. His work since the 1970s has ranged across archaeological theory, radiocarbon dating, the prehistory of language, archaeogenetics and the prevention of looting at archaeological sites. His leadership within the university and public sectors has also been instrumental in the growing position of archaeology in public life.

From the mid-1980s there came a backlash against the prevailing culture of processual archaeology that continues to be influential. A more humanistic approach to the past began to be developed, with the emergence of theories about the past in which scientific models had their place but the complexity of humans was emphasised. These new approaches eventually became unified under the banner of 'post-processual' archaeology, a term that represents an interwoven and sometimes conflicting array of different theoretical approaches to the understanding of past societies that partly rejects the scientifically driven agendas of processual archaeology.

Famous proponents of post-processual archaeology include Ian Hodder (whose work at the Neolithic site of Çatalhöyük in Turkey has been central to the development of many of his theoretical analyses) and, most infamously, Chris Tilley, in his 1991 book *Material Culture and Text*, which has been criticised for suggesting that no amount of archaeological data can compensate for the impact of modern biases, such as personal opinions and experiences, on our analysis of archaeological sites and materials. Such extreme variants of post-processual archaeology – effectively suggesting that the past is basically unknowable, since past human behaviour is too random and different from modern society ever to be understood, let alone modelled – have now been abandoned. In their place has emerged, since the mid 1990s, a more nuanced approach that takes the best of processual and post-processual, scientific and humanist approaches to archaeology, to attempt as full an understanding of past societies as possible.

Post-processual archaeological dialogues have played a role in the discipline beyond seemingly arcane philosophical debates. From these dialogues have come new approaches to gender, class and other determinants of social relations; a politicisation of archaeology that raises questions about inclusivity within the discipline on the grounds of gender, sexuality, race, class and other social markers. Also associated with these dialogues was the involvement of archaeology in broader political debates, such as the political right of Indigenous communities around the world to control their lives, lands and cultural property, and the relationship of archaeologists working in or for politically restrictive regimes, such as archaeologists in South Africa under the apartheid regime. The archaeologist Peter Ucko (1938–2007) was a leader of such widening approaches to world archaeology, particularly through his leadership of the World Archaeological Congress, which was set up in 1986 in response to apartheid policies.

The practical and theoretical expansion of the 1950s, '60s and '70s meant that by the early 1980s global archaeology was in a far stronger position than it had ever been. The formal protection of archaeological sites was at least partially in place in many countries, alongside an informal career structure. Training and research facilities abounded by the 1980s, together with practical and theoretical techniques and approaches of a startling variety. Alongside these formal developments, public interest in archaeology was extremely high, with thousands of active volunteer and charitable archaeological organisations. The Council for British Archaeology (founded in 1944) and its offshoot the Young Archaeologists Club (founded in 1972) are two examples of the kinds of community archaeology organisations that exist around the world.

By the mid-1980s, the worst losses of archaeological sites due to developments such as new buildings or roads had largely ended, thanks to intense lobbying for improved protection and state funding. However, most countries still did not have a formal system of legal protection of archaeological sites. A lot of 'rescue' projects only happened because local archaeological societies or other organisations undertook the work, often at the last minute and with insecure or inconsistent funding. Only in the late 1980s did the principle of 'polluter pays' funding begin to be applied more consistently: that is, that a developer of a new building, road or other development should pay the costs of any archaeological work needed as a consequence of their development.

The last twenty years of archaeology have seen relatively less change than the previous twenty years, although the challenging global economic circumstances since 2007 have forced a major realignment. In many ways, the recent history of archaeology is most distinctive in how archaeology has entered the mainstream and so been affected by the same general trends as the rest of society, rather than existing in a niche. In part this is to do with the democratisation of information that the mass media, and especially the Internet, have enabled. It is now far easier for people to find out about and become involved in archaeology. Thanks to television programmes and even entire 'heritage' television channels, archaeology is a part of mainstream media in a way it never previously was.

Some of the greatest changes in archaeology over the past twenty years have come from external developments, in particular technological developments. As for everyone, advances in computing capacity, speed and complexity, as well as portability and reliability, have revolutionised archaeologists' lives, making it easier to not only collect, collate and analyse large and complex data sets but also to share that data and the resulting analyses. In other respects, archaeology since about 1990 has been very much 'business as usual'. Practical as well as theoretical tools have not changed as much as might have been expected; nor, in general terms, have management, legal, funding and institutional structures.

What has been the defining characteristic of archaeology over the past twenty or so years is the exponential growth of the discipline around the world. Archaeology in the twenty-first century is a truly global profession. Almost every nation has some professional archaeologists, although no one really knows how many archaeologists there are, as there is no central, global management organisation to record these data. The global growth areas for archaeology in the early twenty-first century are the same as the socio-economic growth and leadership areas: Asia (especially China), the Indian subcontinent, Africa and South and Central America. These regions already have well-established archaeological communities but there is no doubt that they will experience distinctively greater growth and come to relatively greater prominence in future archaeological practice and theory.

2

Tools and techniques

To the average person on the street, archaeology is fundamentally about the physical process of discovering and exploring sites. Different locations may require different tools and techniques but in the popular imagination the objective is generally felt to be the same: to get into the field and, if not actually dig, then at least explore, survey and map. This physical aspect of 'doing' archaeology is the one that attracts most people to the subject, be they amateurs or professionals. But while considering these physical aspects we must also assess the mental dimension to such work. As Professor Henry Jones Jr comments at the start of *Indiana Jones and the Last Crusade*: 'Seventy percent of all archaeology is done in the library. Research. Reading. We cannot afford to take mythology at face value'.

The archaeological process

Archaeologists study the physical remains of ancient societies and create a record of these studies that tell us certain things about past people, often with a great degree of detail and accuracy. They examine what types of houses people lived in, what objects they made, what plants they grew, what influence they had on their landscape and how their landscape influenced their diet, their health and the length of their lives.

Physical, tangible evidence of this type is clearly knowable – and there is less and less guesswork involved as our tools for surveying and recording become ever more accurate. But through the traces that we study, archaeologists also use such data to formulate hypotheses about broader, much less knowable things: ancient peoples' motivations, fears and desires, and how these feelings influenced how they lived their lives. It is this intermixing of the practical and theoretical, the physical and mental, that makes archaeology such an engaging pursuit.

Research objectives

Before beginning any type of fieldwork, archaeologists must first address some serious questions about the process of *doing* archaeology. The archaeologist Mortimer Wheeler, who served as a soldier in both World Wars, explained these concerns in his 1954 book *Archaeology from the Earth*. He drew many analogies with military planning, with which practical archaeology shares similarities. In a modern context, the archaeologist Martin Carver (another former soldier) outlined similar analogies in his 2009 book *Archaeological Investigation*. It is this approach that I shall follow in this book.

Most importantly, archaeologists always have a *reason*, a rationale for undertaking fieldwork. It might be a broad question to do with an overarching research strategy, such as searching for evidence of a particular type of physical activity on a site or region that is under analysis. Alternatively, the rationale might be a more detailed question, to do with the continuing investigation of a smaller area, such as looking at a particular section of an ancient town that has not previously been explored. Very differently, another sound justification for undertaking fieldwork is as a response to a recent, unexpected, new archaeological site or find. Under such circumstances, work may be undertaken to establish how this new discovery fits in with wider questions, such as the understanding of ancient trade routes.

These days, most archaeology – around ninety percent – is undertaken reactively, in advance of construction for new houses, businesses, roads, infrastructure, and so on, rather than as part of a proactive research strategy. None the less, reactive archaeology has just as much of a research agenda as proactive. All reputable archaeology begins with detailed pre-fieldwork analyses that sum up the known evidence for the specific area to be investigated, be it miles or metres in extent. A proactive archaeological project might be able to decide where this area of investigation will be placed, unlike a reactive project, but the process underlying both pieces of work is the same. All good archaeology is driven by a deep understanding of what we already know about the history of an area, and that knowledge, such as the types of materials we anticipate will be discovered or the complexity of the archaeological remains likely to be present, informs subsequent actions on-site.

Desk-based analyses

A vast array of modern and historical documents can be used to inform archaeologists' work before they ever set foot on an actual site. Months, and in some cases years, of desk-based research go into most archaeological projects. Such preliminary research is relatively cheap to undertake and thus helps reduce fieldwork costs and time. Desk-based analyses help to ensure that archaeologists start by looking in the right place when searching for a specific site. Analyses also help in planning the logistics of any fieldwork, identifying things as prosaic as modern power, utility and waste services that may be buried on a site, as well as things such as land ownership and access arrangements.

Desk-based assessments determine, as far as is reasonably possible from existing records, the nature, extent and significance of the historic environment within a specified area. When archaeological work is to be undertaken before the construction of new facilities, desk-based assessments also establish the significance of the impact of a proposed development on the historic environment or identify the need for further evaluation. This enables reasoned proposals and decisions to be made, whether they be to mitigate, offset or accept the impact without further intervention. The five main data sources of desk-based assessments are:

- *Archaeological* – this includes central- and local-government-held records of previous archaeological fieldwork or known historic sites (variously referred to as Sites and Monuments Records (SMRs), Historic Environment Records (HERs), State Heritage Inventories, Records of the Historic Environment and Registers of Historic Places); information held in local, regional or national inventories of historic sites (archaeological sites and historic buildings); marine data for sites such as shipwrecks; and also specific data such as records of aircraft crash sites held by the military.
- *Geological* – this includes geological map and geotechnical data and evidence from previous boreholes driven into an area that provide an understanding of the geological strata of specific locations as well as localised variations in the water table, salinity and so on.
- *Historic mapping* – non-government maps include county maps, estate maps, enclosure maps, tithe maps and land sales maps. In Europe and North America some of these maps, such as John Speed's map series of Britain, date back to the seventeenth century. There is also a range of government-sponsored maps in many nations, for example the Ordnance Survey in the UK, including 1 inch (Old Series), 6 inch (1:10,560 scale), 25 inch (1:2500 scale) and ten foot (1:500 scale) maps.

- *Air photographs* – these include vertical air photos (taken from directly above a site and useful for the creation of maps and plans of a location), oblique photos (taken from an angle and good for identifying features above and below ground, thanks to shadows left by undulations in the ground, frost and parch marks from extreme weather, differential growth rates of plants due to subsurface features and so on) and satellite photos (for example, from Google Earth).
- *Documentary sources* – primary documentary sources include a wide variety of legal deeds, account books, diaries and letters, administrative records, newspapers, drawings, paintings and works of literature. Secondary sources include local histories, archaeological journals, monographs and books and also what is known as 'grey literature' (unpublished data from previous archaeological work in the area held in different archives).

Issues of scale

Archaeology is about people and how the physical traces of people – commonly referred to by archaeologists as 'material culture' – survive in different ways, from tiny objects that an individual made, to entire landscapes that groups of humans transformed. The differentiation of this human impact, from the very smallest of impacts to the very largest, is what archaeologists refer to as 'scale'. Archaeologists ask questions regarding how surviving physical remains reflect these scales of impact. These different scales are used to structure this book: Chapter 3 considers the smallest scale of individual materials and objects, Chapter 4 the medium scale of multiple components and places and Chapters 5 and 6 the largest scale of landscapes and travel across and between them.

The smallest scale of the data for past peoples is that of the tiny traces of flora and fauna that survive in archaeological remains such as old rubbish pits, ditches and drains, which indicate what plant species existed in the past. Sometimes referred to as *ecofacts*, or faunal remains, these materials provide an insight into past environments. Moving up in scale, there is a vast array of variously-sized physical remains of the past, from small, common and workaday materials such as pottery, tools, weapons and toys, to large and very complex machines.

At another level of scale are structures made of multiple components: houses, workplaces, places for ritual or pleasure, or places for specific activities such as bathing. Such structures, and the smaller materials that survive within them, exist within another level of scale: communities, from single houses or complexes such as farms by way of hamlets and villages to towns and cities. Such built environments sit within much larger physical and social territories; environments that provide evidence of ancient sources of food, water and materials but which also reflect less tangible cultural activities, such as political, social or economic influences.

Carrying on up the scale to the largest extent, archaeologists study entire landscapes: the evidence of large-scale human modification of the environment. Some of these landscapes are immediately related to past social structures (for example, an entire ancient kingdom), while others are more immediately connected to identifiable environmental characteristics (for example, a coastline, island, specific type of terrain or evidence of ancient farming). Finally, archaeologists study connections between these places: the evidence of ancient travel, trade, transport and communication.

Measuring time – chronology

Alongside the study of scale, another basic principle of archaeology is the study of time; of dating the past and identifying when and why different events took place in relation to one another. The origins of this type of analysis lie in the beginnings of archaeology, especially its relationship with the science of geology. Nineteenth-century studies of the antiquity of the earth, especially using the study of geological strata (layers), had a profound influence on early archaeology. This, in turn, influenced studies of the origins of the antiquity of humankind and the furore about human evolution that has persisted since the publication of Charles Darwin's book *On the Origin of Species*, first published in 1859.

Until 1949, when radiocarbon (sometimes referred to as Carbon-14 or C14) dating was developed, archaeology's study of chronology was based on what is known as the principle of 'relative' dating – determining the relative order of past events through archaeological excavation without determining the chronometric ('absolute') age of materials. Relative dating is the principle used in geology for analysing different strata. It involves determining the relative order of past events without necessarily determining their absolute age. Understanding the sequential order in which a series of events occurred, not *when* they specifically occurred, remains a useful technique, especially for materials lacking the radioactive isotopes needed for C14 dating; stone, metal and pottery cannot usually be directly dated unless there is some organic material either embedded in them or left as a residue on them.

The key archaeological concepts used in relative dating are referred to by the Latin phrases *terminus post quem* ('limit after which') and *terminus ante quem* ('limit before which'). Such archaeological sites are dated by relative chronologies. This means using materials such as date-stamped coins or distinctive types of pottery to broadly date adjacent layers discovered in the process of an excavation in relation to one another. A useful analogy is the way in which the layers of a multi-tiered wedding cake are put together: the bottom layer of cake has to have been in place before the upper layers were placed on top; the bottom layer is thus relatively older than the upper ones.

On an archaeological site, the discovery of buried coins is one of the most useful ways of providing a relative date for the layers above them. Almost without exception, coins have a date stamp, or some other marker (such as the name of a king, queen or other leader), that can securely date them to a specific time. A coin minted during the reign of the Roman emperor Hadrian (117–138 CE) has to date from that 21-year period: it cannot have been buried before 117 CE. If a coin of Hadrian is found in an archaeological layer, anything found above the coin has to date from *after* 117 CE (the *terminus post quem*). If we're really lucky, the coin might bear a specific date, further narrowing the range.

However, relative dating only works going forwards, not backwards. A coin minted between 117 and 138 CE can only have been buried after 117 CE but it could have been buried *at any time* between or after that date range; perhaps as recently as a day, week or month ago. Archaeologists discovering such a coin must pay close attention to the materials surrounding it to try to identify the context of its burial: how, perhaps when, and even why the coin was buried.

Relative dating relies on a series of 'laws of stratigraphy'. This is an archaeological adaptation of the geological model that the earth's layers of rock were laid down in uniform, observable patterns. The laws were developed by archaeologists from the late nineteenth century onwards but were formalised in 1979 in the work of the archaeologist Edward Harris, in his book *Principles of Archaeological Stratigraphy*:

- The *principle of superposition* – in a series of layers as originally created, the upper layers are younger and the lower are older, for each must have been deposited on, or created by the removal of, a pre-existing mass of archaeological stratification.

- The *principle of original horizontality* – any archaeological layer will tend towards a horizontal disposition.
- The *principle of original continuity* – any archaeological deposit as originally created will be bounded by the edge of a basin of deposition (a lip) or will thin down to a 'feather' edge.
- *The principle of stratigraphic succession* – any given unit of archaeological stratification takes its place in the stratigraphic sequence of a site from its position between the under-most of all units that lie above it and the uppermost of all those units that lie below it and with which it has physical contact.

Harris not only formalised archaeologists' understanding of the key principles of relative dating through sequences but also provided a means of recording these relationships, in what has become known as the 'Harris Matrix'. The matrix is a diagrammatic tool used to depict the temporal succession of archaeological 'contexts' (that is, the different layers and other discrete features of a site, such as post holes and pits). As shown in Figure 1, each different context is given a unique reference number (for example, context 308 is a Victorian 'cut', context 341, a timber drain) that can be shown on a diagram in relation to all other contexts. Such sequences can run, on complex and deeply stratified sites, to tens of thousands of individual contexts but, despite their complexity, they are extremely useful diagrammatic representations of archaeological sites, since they provide a simplified diagram of all the interrelationships of the different components of any archaeological site.

In Figure 1, the most modern layers are at the top of the image (262 is the modern ground surface). The image runs down to the oldest layers (373 and 366 are the first layers of human activity that overlie the original, natural, unaltered ground surface, 042). The different boxes depict major features; in this case, a series of pits that overlie one another and were filled in at different stages

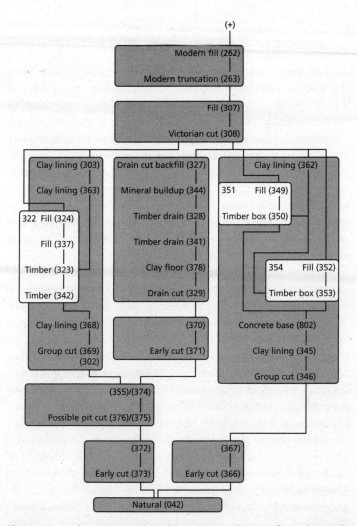

Figure 1 Harris matrix stratigraphic sequence diagram from the medieval Wild's Rents tannery, Bermondsey, London (copyright and courtesy of Archaeology South-East)

in the past. The separate numbered elements reflect specific layers within each of these features. The vertical and horizontal lines depict the connections between each feature.

The matrix system also helps archaeological site management systems, especially the principle of 'single context recording', in which the different contexts are not only given a unique reference number but also a unique record of their shape, size, content and other characteristics, logged using pro forma records, including diagrams, sketches and photographs. Such methods of recording ensure that all the information discovered during an archaeological excavation is consistently recorded and available for future study (proof of the principle that since all archaeological excavation is a destructive process, we must preserve 'by record' when we excavate, leaving as comprehensive a record of our work as possible in the place of the actual archaeology).

A principle related to stratigraphy, used to date materials rather than archaeological sites, is *typology*. Typology is used by many disciplines in both the sciences and humanities to study different types of materials and their interrelationships. In archaeology it refers to the classification of materials in relation to changes in their characteristics over time, a form of relative dating in which variations in the typological characteristics of different materials are linked by association to other datable materials. The principle of typology is most often used in archaeology to study sequences of different types of ceramics through the analysis of changes in their shape, especially their rim shape and decoration, over time. A familiar analogy of this approach is the typology of the petrol-driven motor vehicle. Since their invention in 1885 by Karl Benz, the design of motor vehicles has changed periodically in distinctive blocks, especially since the end of the Second World War. From its shape, most people could identify a car from the 1950s, 1960s, 1970s, 1980s, and so on. All are motor vehicles but the variations in their relative shapes are extremely distinctive and tied to quite tight times. Similar typologies can be created for all sorts of modern materials, from soft drinks bottles and cans to lamp posts or postboxes.

The development of radiocarbon dating, the first and still most commonly used of the scientific techniques that make up chronometric (absolute) dating techniques, transformed global archaeology. It led to a re-dating of many archaeological sites and the revision – in some cases outright rebuttal – of many assumptions and hypotheses about the chronology of ancient societies. The ability to precisely and accurately date archaeological layers and materials gives a chronological security that has allowed much closer relationships to be drawn between archaeological sites, refining our understanding of the sequence of events in the past.

'Raw', or uncalibrated, radiocarbon ages are usually reported in radiocarbon years 'Before Present' (BP), in which 'present' is set at 1950 CE. Such raw ages can then be calibrated to give more specific calendar dates with a likely upper and lower date range and an indication of degree of accuracy. For example, an object might be given a date of '2200 +/- 50 years BP', meaning its sampled materials date from between 2150 and 2250 years BP; that is, around 200–300 BCE, the latter days of the Roman Republic in north-west Europe.

In archaeology, radiocarbon dating is most frequently used to estimate the age of organic remains. In nature, most carbon exists as two stable, non-radioactive isotopes, Carbon-12 and Carbon-13, with a tiny proportion being the radioactive isotope Carbon-14. Radiocarbon dating uses the levels of Carbon-14 (C14) present in a sample to estimate the age of carbon-bearing materials. When plants turn atmospheric carbon dioxide into sugars during photosynthesis, this sugar will include a quantity of C14 that approximately matches its level in the atmosphere at that time. When the plants die, or are consumed by other organisms (for example, by humans or other animals), the accumulation of carbon stops and the quantity of C14 present declines at a

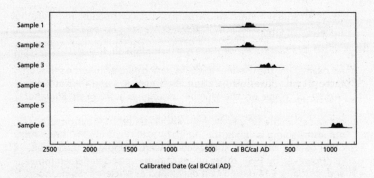

Figure 2 C14 probability distributions of dates from Brisley Farm, Ashford, Kent (copyright and courtesy of Archaeology South-East)

fixed rate, due to the process of radioactive decay. Comparing the remaining fraction of C14 in a sample of an ancient material to that expected in atmospheric C14 allows the age of the ancient sample to be estimated. As shown in Figure 2, a series of samples can then be compared to one another to provide a date range for the site in question.

In Figure 2, the date range runs along the bottom of the diagram; the series of six different materials sampled using C14 dating are listed along the left-hand side and their date ranges run left–right across the diagram, providing an overall date range for the site. For example, the longest date range comes from sample 5, with a calibrated date range from 2200 BCE to 300 BCE but with a peak (most likely) calibrated date of 1300–1100 BCE).

The sensitivity of radiocarbon dating has been greatly increased of late by the use of accelerator mass spectrometry (AMS). Using this technique, C14 atoms are detected and counted directly, as opposed to detecting radioactive decay, as was the practice. This method allows the dating of samples containing only a few milligrams of carbon, meaning that a much smaller sample of any datable material needs to be used by archaeologists.

RADIOCARBON DATING IN ACTION: THE NORTH FERRIBY BOATS

An example of the usefulness of C14 dating comes from the series of three prehistoric vessels discovered between 1937 and 1963 at North Ferriby, a village on the Humber estuary in north-east England. When the first boat was discovered in 1937, C14 dating techniques did not exist: the vessel was typologically dated to the Bronze Age, but establishing a more specific date was not possible, since no other datable materials, such as coins, were found with the vessels.

However, by 1958, other pieces of these vessels had been found and, crucially, C14 dating had developed as a science. Some wood and twine from the site were successfully dated, yielding a more specific date of 750 +/- 150 BCE, in the Later Bronze Age. More recently, the refinement of C14 dating has allowed much more precise measurements to be undertaken. In 2001 the Ferriby boats were publicly acclaimed as Europe's earliest sea craft, a refinement that caused a rethink about the nature of pan-European technology, trade and exchange in this period. The new C14 analyses dated boat one to 1880–1680 BCE, boat two to 1940–1720 BCE and boat three to 2030–1780 BCE.

Over more than sixty years, a site first discovered in the 1930s by a local man, Ted Wright, while walking along a beach with his brother and his pet dogs, has been more and more accurately dated thanks to C14 analyses. These analyses have demonstrated the international significance of these finds, which are arguably the most important prehistoric ship finds in north-west Europe.

Absolute dating techniques such as C14 dating have helped demonstrate both that biologically modern humans were active far longer ago than had previously been thought, and that they had a high degree of technological sophistication. Radiocarbon dating proved conclusively that humans colonised Australia by sea from south-east Asia at least forty to fifty thousand years ago; tens of thousands of years earlier than had previously been thought. Before radiocarbon dating, archaeologists had hypothesised, using the limited evidence offered by relative dating, that people had been present in Australia for only a few thousand years. The expansion of the global time-depth of the human race, and its worldwide presence, enabled by the radiocarbon revolution was transformative, forcing our entire understanding of the technological sophistication of ancient societies to be redrawn. Since that time, more and more sophisticated types of carbon dating, as well as other techniques of absolute scientific dating, have been developed and continue to refine our understanding of global chronology.

Recent advances in scientific analysis complement the evidence for the antiquity and origins of the human race that we have collected from absolute dating techniques. Most notable is the use of genetic analyses of modern populations to trace the presence of ancestral DNA in different locations, which has helped strengthen our understanding of the prehistoric global peopling of the world. A good example of this is research carried out at Stanford University since 2011, in which a team from the Stanford Genome Technology Center has pioneered a technique to trace historic genetic variations in the Y chromosome of living men. The Y chromosome is the sex chromosome that encodes maleness; males have one Y chromosome (from their father) and one X chromosome (from their mother), while females have two X chromosomes (one from each parent). Y chromosomes change very little from one generation to the next; furthermore, in men, only a tiny region of the Y chromosome can swap DNA with the X chromosome. This means that almost all of a Y chromosome moves intact from father to son, changing only infrequently when a new mutation arises.

The Stanford team analysed Y chromosomes from men in thirteen populations, in Tanzania in eastern Africa and in the Namibia-Botswana-Angola border region of southern Africa. These populations were over 2000 km apart. The researchers identified a mutation shared by some men in *both* locations, which implied that the men had a common ancestor. Further analysis showed the mutation arose in eastern Africa about ten thousand years ago and was carried by migration to southern Africa about two thousand years ago. This genetic evidence correlates well with archaeological evidence and also explains linguistic similarities between the peoples in the two regions.

For archaeologists, the significance of such studies is threefold. First, the ability to use modern DNA to trace ancient patterns of migration makes research easier; it is much harder to look for ancient DNA data on archaeological sites than it is to sample the DNA of living humans. Second, the ability to track migrations offers an insight into ancient patterns of movement and thus into cognition as well as technology; both how and potentially why people moved to different locations. Third, if such a pattern can be identified in one location in Africa, the technique may work in other locations for other populations, such as tracking similar ancient movements elsewhere in Africa, the Americas, Asia or Australasia.

Data types and availability

Archaeologists need to verify, as accurately as is possible, that the location they intend to explore contains the data they wish to collect. This may sound obvious, but archaeology is an inexact science. There is always a balance between the known and the unknown: what is already known about a site or area and so what might reasonably be predicted in terms of future discoveries versus the impact of random chance and unexpected discovery. Archaeologists try to ascertain, as much as they can, what has previously been found in a place and so predict what might be found in the future. This part of the research process underlies fieldwork but it is also about minimising risk and making sure that fieldwork is as effective as possible. This links with the related, and core, area of project planning.

Archaeological planning is driven by a combination of factors, beginning with the underlying research objectives and moving on through the issues of availability of data, scale, logistics and post-fieldwork planning. One of the worst mistakes made by many archaeological projects in the past has been underestimating both the amount and sensitivity of any materials recovered and so underestimating how much post-excavation conservation of materials would be needed. Materials recovered from waterlogged sites, for example, can often include very delicate organic materials like leather and cloth, which tell a tremendous amount about past lives but which are extremely sensitive and expensive to conserve and display.

Scale and sampling

In terms of data collection, issues of scale and sampling, and therefore statistics and research strategy, play a major part in fieldwork organisation. Planning means understanding what research questions underlie a proposed piece of fieldwork and the type(s) of data that will be necessary to help answer these questions. Part of planning is estimating the type and range of archaeological materials that will be discovered and thus the types of excavation and preservation approaches that will have to be used. A dry site yielding stone tools and pottery will require very different approaches to a wet site full of organic remains such as ancient wood, leather and fabric.

Planning also means identifying how much data will need to be collected over what area; that is, the physical amount of land that must be explored to produce a statistically relevant dataset. Most samples will cover at best 10–15% of the total area of any site; the upper limit on a few sites might be 40–50%. These decisions influence the overall strategy of the project; that is, what will be done when and in what order. In a few exceptional circumstances, the whole of a single archaeological site might be excavated and so such questions are less relevant; the sample, scale and statistics will be entirely influenced by the existing archaeological remains. But such large-scale fieldwork is unusual. Even when they do happen, excavations of such a large size almost inevitably take place over several years; often a decade or more for bigger sites. Consequently, such projects still require planning in terms of the systematic process of exploration, prioritising different areas for each phase of excavation.

THE ARCHAEOLOGY OF GARBAGE

The Tucson Garbage Project saw the application of archaeological techniques to *modern* buried materials; in this case, landfill open-cast garbage dumps around the city of Tucson, Arizona, USA. From 1973 onwards, the project, led by the archaeologist William Rathje (1945–2012) highlighted the fallibility of written records in comparison to the archaeological record. Quantitative data from landfill garbage, recovered under controlled, scientific circumstances – an archaeological excavation – was compared with information known about the residents who had disposed of the garbage and information derived from broader social data collected on the households and their neighbourhoods. The results demonstrated that what people admit about their consumption habits does not necessarily correspond to the contents of their rubbish bins when the reality is observed by studying their garbage. For example, alcohol consumption was found to be much higher than the participants admitted in the questionnaires they completed.

Projects such as this demonstrate a number of key issues relating to the analysis and understanding of past human behaviour. Above all, such projects reveal that there can be a gap between people's self-reported and actual behaviour, calling into question the reliability of the historical record when applied to archaeological sites. This dichotomy is especially important in locations where archaeological sites have surviving associated documents.

In the past, the assumption was that surviving documentary records rendered archaeological investigations superfluous. The Garbage Project demonstrated that archaeology offers an alternative perspective on the past, especially as regards people's behaviour.

This is true on all sorts of sites, from the very ancient, thousands of years old, to the very new, hundreds or tens of years old.

The classic work on the use of such historical archaeology is the American archaeologist James Deetz's (1930–2000) 1977 book, *In Small Things Forgotten: An Archaeology of Early American Life*. Deetz, through his studies of a number of seventeenth-, eighteenth- and nineteenth-century sites in America, especially in and around New England, demonstrated the significance of a range of small recovered objects for our understanding of the daily life of past societies. Deetz explored the details of everything from the structure of doorways, to changes in the design of gravestones, to types of clay pipe. In the same way as the Tucson Garbage Project, he used this panoply of evidence to reveal underlying social mores and structures that historical documents alone, even though they survive for such communities, are often incapable of identifying. In particular, Deetz's work helped to better acknowledge the presence of women and African Americans in early Colonial America, two communities that are often nearly invisible in the documentary record but which can be identified through archaeology.

From discovery to publication

The basic principles of practical archaeology come from outside the archaeological community and are applied by people all the time: the 'five Ws' of *who, what, when, where* and *why*.

In archaeological fieldwork, a special pressure comes from the fact that excavation inevitably involves the destruction of a finite, non-renewable resource: the physical remains of the past. The destructive nature of archaeological excavation should cause all involved to hesitate during project planning and ask themselves: 'is excavation necessary *at all*?' Could the question be answered through other, non-destructive means, such as non-invasive surveys, remote sensing or the re-analysis of data collected by other people? Archaeologists try not to excavate unless strictly necessary and, when they do, they ensure that they undertake the most destructive work carefully, within the ethos of preservation by record. Archaeologists also ensure that this record is publicly available.

Logistical concerns – the detail of making sure a project actually works, is on time, within budget and gets the job done – are important components of practical archaeology. No archaeological project in the history of the subject has ever had enough time, money or resources. Careful logistics makes the maximum use of limited resources. Archaeological logistics can be broken down into a series of points that runs from identifying and surveying the site in advance, to fieldwork, to the post-excavation stage, via ensuring supplies of equipment, food, fuel and other essentials. Crucially, in this respect, the end of archaeological fieldwork is the start of a new cycle of 'post-excavation' work. This means everything from stabilising and conserving any materials recovered (including possibly preparing them for display in a museum) to publishing and promoting the discoveries through books, online media, radio or television. Post-fieldwork activities take many years; frequently many times the length of the fieldwork and at many times the cost.

Planning also requires identifying in advance – and finding the financial support for – the costs of all this work. Such costs include having a suitable place and facilities to undertake scientific analyses, storing materials, paying for people to undertake conservation and analytical work, and publicising and publishing the results. Logistics also involves getting appropriate legal permission to work on a site, whether from national and local authorities or landowners; this last group is particularly important. Close liaison with local communities is also crucial, whether in directly involving the community in planning and running a project, in offering public open days, talks and events, or simply in terms of the archaeologists being a part of a community for a time, ensuring that a large project is no nuisance to people going about their daily lives.

Finding sites

Finding sites depends on the very nature of archaeological discovery itself: proactive versus reactive strategies. Many archaeological sites are discovered in the course of other human activity such as the construction of new buildings, roads and other infrastructure. Such 'reactive' archaeology is the driving force of the majority of archaeological work in many countries. An archaeological site is discovered during some other activity and is investigated with regard to local, national or international research questions relating to other archaeological sites both near and far. It is still a process of research and investigation but is driven by factors beyond the archaeologists' immediate control.

A smaller percentage of sites is discovered as a result of 'proactive' research strategies, by archaeologists seeking sites to answer specific questions. In this process, archaeologists draw on a variety of existing data to hypothesise where the types of sites they are interested in might lie, undiscovered. The archaeologists will search for patterns: distribution patterns of similar types of site or particular types of materials associated with specific activities. The archaeologists will also draw on geographic and geological data, examining environmental and topographic data, such as distinctive types of soil or the presence of fresh water, which might indicate the presence of a settlement.

Archaeologists also use different types of sampling and modelling strategies, including statistical models, to plan and implement fieldwork. These strategies can be used, for example, to set up statistically meaningful sampling criteria to identify the location of different sites in a landscape to be surveyed or excavated. Once the archaeologists have 'homed in' on sites in this way, similar techniques might help to decide how much material or data, and what types of data, need to be recovered from each site to help build up a hypothetical model of human behaviour there.

Surveying sites

Assuming that a site, or even a discrete area, has been identified as containing archaeological features worthy of investigation,
one type of archaeological work involves undertaking detailed
surveys. These are usually 'non-invasive', in that they generally do
not involve excavation, but are more physical, in the sense that
they involve groups of people moving across the landscape and
recording it in detail, unlike the remote sensing discussed later
in this chapter. In many cases such surveys are all that is needed;
a survey can be a complete project on its own and need not be
followed by invasive excavation.

Many excavations undertake such surveys in advance of invasive fieldwork. In some cases they may be undertaken over a relatively small area: a few hundred or thousand square metres over
adjoining fields, or along a particular stretch of a road or river.
In other cases, the survey may be on a large scale, over tens or
even hundreds of square miles, to provide rich data for a whole
landscape.

LANDSCAPE SURVEY ON KYTHERA ISLAND

The Kythera Island Project (KIP), run between 1998 and 2001 by
the Institute of Archaeology in London, is an excellent example
of an intensive landscape survey. Four seasons of surveying took
place on the island, one of the Ionian Islands in Greece. The project
concentrated on the central-eastern region of Kythera, covering
a spectrum of landscapes from the coast to the island's interior
plateau. In total, the survey area covered 100 km² of the island,
approximately thirty-six percent of its surface area.

Within the survey area, 43 km² were intensively surveyed in
sub-hectare tracts (with a median size of 0.4ha, approximately one
acre) by walkers spaced 15 m apart. The tract walking was designed
to sample the survey area in regular, 1 km-wide, north–south tran-
sects. This enabled the team to explore a variety of cultural and

environmental locations while simultaneously covering regions of special interest, such as portions of the coastline and well-preserved or agriculturally-favoured areas of the interior. The surveyors worked in teams of four to seven, each individually recording pottery counts, lithics (worked stone objects), metal débris and distance walked. Additional diagnostic pottery, lithics and metal-lurgical débris were collected for further study, alongside support-ing information including ground surface visibility, land use and vegetation, and standing and rock-cut features.

Using such apparently simple but intensive methods, the project documented and analysed about two hundred archaeologi-cal sites. The fieldwork enabled the long-term dynamics of insular-ity to be better understood; that is, the cultural and environmental history of an ostensibly closed island community. Kythera's loca-tion makes it a stepping stone for maritime movement between Crete and the Peloponnese. Far from being an isolated and insular community, Kythera was a crucial node between the Aegean and the central Mediterranean. The field surveys reflected the changing nature – especially the changing location and density – of this activ-ity. Life on ancient Kythera was influenced by engagement with a variety of off-island networks of differing nature and extent, including Bronze Age Cretan palatial trade routes, the hegemony of Iron Age Sparta and the empires of Athens, Rome, Byzantium, Venice, Ottoman Turkey and finally Britain, until unification with the modern Greek state.

Landscape surveys can encompass many different approaches and tools. The most basic is 'field walking'; literally, groups of people strung in a line walking across a landscape and search-ing for archaeological traces such as pieces of broken pottery or the outlines of walls or buildings. Such surveys work particularly well on farmland that has been recently ploughed, which reveals fragments of pottery and other scattered remains. The quanti-ties and densities of materials recovered can be carefully mapped, measured, weighed and recorded to build up detailed maps that can then be subjected to statistical analyses, highlighting locations with lots of archaeological features.

A more destructive version of such work is 'test pitting': exca-vating (normally) one-metre-square pits either along a line or at set, or sometimes random, distances around an area to identify archaeological remains. In the USA and Australia, test pitting is often undertaken along the route of new roads or pipelines. In such cases, the test pits may be placed every few hundred metres for hundreds of miles. A compromise is measured 'coring' along a route, taking much smaller samples using a hand-driven or powered auger.

Test-pit surveys are a less common approach in countries such as the UK where the intensity of human occupation offers its own means of survey. However, specific villages have been usefully test pitted in the UK, not to identify the general presence of archaeological evidence but rather the breadth and depth of past human activity, highlighting how towns and villages developed and changed over time.

REMOTE SENSING

Often simply referred to as 'geophys', the best known and most widely used of the various types of land-based remote sensing are resistivity and magnetometer surveys.

Resistivity surveys send an electric current through the earth between a series of probes inserted into the land and a survey stand inserted at regular intervals. When the stand is inserted into the earth the electrical circuit between the probes and the stand is completed and the current can be measured. Local variations in the current indicate different features; elements such as buried walls slow the current while others, such as former (now buried) ditches, allow it to flow more easily. In comparison, magnetometer surveys record local variations in the earth's magnetic field: traces of ancient activities, such as the sites of fires or deposits of metal, create local 'hotspots' of increased magnetism.

In both methods, the operator takes thousands of readings by walking up and down measured lines of a survey area in a strict order, taking a measurement every metre or less. The data is sent to a computer, which analyses it to slowly reveal the details of what is buried beneath. Some post-processing cleaning of the image to enhance the record is usually needed.

Both resistivity and magnetometer surveys are time-consuming; a single large field may take a day to survey. Post-processing may take even longer, as well as requiring relatively expensive equipment and specialised, trained operators. Both systems do not work under certain conditions; different types of geology, or even the land being too wet or dry, can spoil or prevent a survey. But under the right circumstances the outcome can be dramatic, providing a detailed digital map of a site that can be used to precisely place excavation trenches over specific locations to help maximise the investigation.

A related technique is ground-penetrating radar (GPR). This sends high-frequency pulses of radio waves into the ground from a survey machine pulled along the surface. A detector picks up the signals reflected from subsurface features, especially voids and cavities, building up a computerised image of what lies beneath. GPR is more expensive and time-consuming than the other geophysical tools, and is most commonly used on smaller areas with known archaeological features. It is especially useful in identifying the subsurface layout of current and former buildings, such as the subfloor areas of historic churches, where crypts and burial chambers may lie undiscovered.

Archaeology is just as interested in the big picture; questions that are answered not by a specific site or even a single location but in an entire landscape tens, hundreds or even thousands of square miles in extent. In such cases, archaeologists may turn to large-scale remote sensing to identify sites and features. Increasingly this means the use of satellite reconnaissance data.

Once the preserve of the military, satellite imagery is now publicly available from online sources such as Google Earth; more detailed data can also often be purchased for a relatively low price from satellite survey companies. Many previously unknown archaeological sites have been discovered through these means by archaeologists carefully poring over the data to look for the patterns and faint traces of past human activity. Comparable data also exists for the seas and oceans, mapping in detail many millions of square miles of the world's seabeds.

Advances in satellite survey technology are increasingly useful to archaeology. In particular, infrared surveys are capable of identifying long-buried features invisible to the naked eye. One example comes from Egypt, where more than a thousand tombs and three thousand ancient settlements were revealed by a survey of infrared satellite images led by the Egyptologist Sarah Parcak, from the University of Alabama, between 2000 and 2004. Her team analysed images from satellites equipped with cameras powerful enough to pinpoint objects less than one metre in diameter. Infrared imaging was used to highlight different materials under the surface. The data supported more precise survey and excavation work on land, saving time and money.

A different use of satellite surveys comes in the exploration of extremely inaccessible areas. For example, in Siberia, 3D satellite images have been used to help understand landscapes and archaeological sites that, because of the area's remoteness and extreme weather, would take days to reach and months to explore using conventional means. Similarly, satellite surveys have been used on the island of Rapa Nui (Easter Island) to map the roads on which its renowned statues were originally transported.

Archaeologists also use aerial photos – some collected by archaeologists themselves, others by industry and the military – in a similar fashion to satellite imagery. Such photos can be very useful in identifying sites even in relatively well-studied areas, especially photos taken by archaeologists at relatively low heights and at particular times of the day or year, when the light is in the right direction and elements such as the density of plant cover reveal subtle traces of past human activity.

Archaeologists are increasingly using various types of airborne survey technology in the search for sites. LIDAR (LIght Detection And Ranging) airborne laser surveys scan the surface of the land in incredible detail, producing high-density digital maps of the land that can reveal tiny variations. LIDAR also allows different layers, for example plant cover, to be added to or taken away from a digital map, revealing the underlying topography. Such survey tools are very useful in identifying archaeological sites in heavily-forested regions.

Allied to land- and air-based remote sensing is the increasingly important field of marine surveying. Collected by the military, as well as industrial organisations such as oil and gas companies, oceanographic survey data is derived from various different types of marine geophysical survey. These are mainly based on the principles of sonar: projecting sound waves at different frequencies and intensities down into the ocean and recording their rate of return after they have bounced off subsea features, to produce 3D maps of the seafloor.

For archaeologists, an extremely useful variation of sonar is high-resolution 3D Chirp sub-bottom profiling. 3D Chirp is a surface-towed sub-bottom profiling system, based on the principles of sonar but capable of imaging the subsurface of the seabed in three dimensions, with high-resolution horizontal (to one tenth of a metre, that is, 10 cm units) and vertical (to one hundredth of a metre, that is, 1 cm units) data accuracy. The result is a detailed 3D model of the layers beneath the seabed, revealing in detail any buried historic materials. 3D chirp systems can be used in almost any depth of water, as long as it is deep enough to float a survey vessel, and have been used to identify everything from shallow-water prehistoric settlement sites in the Baltic to modern shipwreck sites in the deep ocean.

A different variation of sonar technology also useful to archaeology is high-resolution multi-beam sonar. This technology blends multi-beam sonar, motion reference and subsea positioning systems to visualise underwater archaeological sites in high resolution. Such detailed 3D sonar surveys have been undertaken on a number of notable historic maritime sites, including the wrecks of the German High Seas Fleet in Scapa Flow and wrecks from the Battle of the Atlantic off the Outer Banks of North

AUTONOMOUS UNDERWATER VEHICLES AND MARITIME ARCHAEOLOGY

The most recent advance in archaeological oceanography is the use of Autonomous Underwater Vehicles (AUVs) to survey sites. In 2005, the Greek Ministry of Culture invited a team from the Woods Hole Oceanographic Institution (WHOI) and the Massachusetts Institute of Technology to survey an ancient shipwreck in the Aegean Sea, which lay deeper than divers could safely work. The team used WHOI's SeaBED AUV to document the wreck with digital still cameras and a high-resolution mapping sonar. Over two days, the AUV performed four missions on the site, repeatedly mapping and imaging the wreck. In the first three-hour mission, SeaBED's multi-beam sonar completely mapped the wreck while the digital camera simultaneously collected thousands of high-resolution images. Later the same day, the team assembled those images into photomosaic strips, giving the archaeologists their first overall views of the wreck. Successive missions on the site provided photographs of the wreck from different angles, revealing more detail. In two days, the surveys undertook fieldwork that would have taken a team of conventional human divers, using highly specialised deep-diving equipment, months or even years to complete.

Carolina. Multi-beam sonar systems produce millions of data-points which – when processed together with positioning data – allow the building of detailed 3D images of the features surveyed. Particularly for large, upstanding, metal shipwrecks, the result is colour images so detailed that they look like artists' reconstructions or models, rather than highly accurate surveys.

Excavation

For many people, the ultimate archaeological activity is excavation: physically digging into a site. Thanks to countless television programmes and films this activity, above all others, is what most people think that most archaeologists do most of the time. The reality is almost the opposite: plenty of archaeological projects never involve any physical excavation; they either collect the data needed to answer a question from existing records or use non-invasive techniques.

The reason for the relative lack of excavation is partly to do with the fact that excavation is destruction, so should not be undertaken lightly. There is also the secondary fact that excavation is expensive in money, resources and time. Done well, excavation can reveal things about human behaviour in the past that no other type of investigation can. Done badly, excavation leads only to the damage or destruction of priceless archaeological materials, with little or no benefit.

The biggest question that has to be asked on any potential archaeological site is what *type* of excavation is to be undertaken. The project director may be free to decide this, or it may be determined by external factors beyond his or her control. Some sites' restrictive layouts, such as the construction sites of new buildings in crowded cities, mean that only a small portion of the whole archaeological site can be explored, perhaps a few narrow trenches studied over a few days or weeks. In contrast, a rural excavation undertaken in advance of a new road or pipeline might entail a wide scatter of much larger trenches stretched along the line of the development, over hundreds or thousands of metres, to attempt to interpret the broad layout and extent of the archaeological site.

A lucky few archaeological projects have the luxury of being research-led, exploring a new site with no external factors, and so are able to undertake what is known as 'open area' excavation. This involves stripping off the earth over a single large area of the archaeological site to reveal its full extent, and excavating down through all the layers in order, rather than selectively investigating smaller, isolated trenches. Open area excavation is, however, time-consuming and expensive, not least in terms of the quantity of data it produces and the materials it recovers. The data and materials may take many years to analyse after the excavation itself has finished.

Deciding what type of excavation to undertake is merely one of a multitude of logistical decisions that have to be made well in advance of any fieldwork, in some cases months or even years in advance. Beyond any archaeological considerations, the basic prosaic plans needed to make a project work include:

- *Staff and staff structure/chain of command*, especially if large numbers of students or volunteers will be involved. This includes planning accommodation, catering, health and safety requirements and insurance.
- *Travel arrangements and logistics:* how to get staff and equipment to and from the site, either bringing it all from outside or hiring equipment nearby.
- *Site equipment, layout and logistics*, including issues such as accommodation, cleaning and office space; many archaeological projects involve people camping nearby, with a portable building or caravan as a site office. It also includes planning how to close down the project at the end: carefully backfilling trenches, replacing turf, taking away the equipment and getting the data and staff safely home.
- *Environmental and specialist requirements*, if the project is in a location that requires specific equipment and/or logistics. Examples include very dry or very wet sites (including coastal or underwater sites and deserts), very high and/or remote sites (such as mountain regions, where the air may be thinner) or sites with complicated access or environmental issues (for example, jungles, where there may be dangerous animals and insects).
- *Legal requirements*, including gaining permission from landowners, Indigenous or ancestral communities, or local and national government to access a site, and work permits and visas to enter and work in a country. Many countries have

Figure 3 Excavations under way in advance of a city-centre redevelopment at Eastgate Square, Chichester (copyright and courtesy of Archaeology South-East)

very tight rules regarding the precise permissions needed to undertake archaeological fieldwork, especially for foreigners.

- *Public engagement plans*: most sites can expect at least some visitors and many see hundreds or even thousands. These visitors have to be anticipated, site tours and open days planned and advertised, facilities, including toilets, provided, and parking and access discussed with local residents, landowners and the police, so as to not cause a nuisance. Public engagement may include things such as having a display about the project in a local school, library or museum, involving local schoolchildren in the project, or liaising with the press about reporting.

Specific archaeological considerations include the overall project plans and equipment needs; that is, the type of excavation, type of recording system to be used and provision of pro forma recording sheets. Clear plans must be established for what type and how many diagrams or photos will be taken, by whom and under what circumstances. Plans also need to be made for specialist work and equipment requirements, for example, particular types of survey to be undertaken, any specialist equipment needed, or particular types of environmental or scientific recording required. This part of the planning is also likely to include dedicated plans for the handling, storage and recording of finds.

A topographic survey, that is, recording all the lumps and bumps on the site, will be conducted before as well as during any excavation. Nowadays this involves the use of computerised survey devices known as total stations, which are linked up to a Global Positioning System (GPS) device. Total stations allow detailed and accurate measurements of a site and the precise positioning of features. Once such a survey has been undertaken, these data can in turn be used to create a 'site grid', a map of the site on which all the features discovered are plotted, in some cases down to the level of the precise locations of individual items discovered. The site grid will also be used to help decide exactly where individual trenches will be placed and in turn ensure that these are properly aligned, that is, with exact lengths, widths and right-angled corners, to aid accurate record-keeping.

Having decided what type of excavation to undertake, sorted out the logistics to get people and equipment to the site, and carefully mapped it, only *then* can excavation begin. In many parts of the world this process begins with the careful removal of any turf, which is kept to one side so that it can be replaced at the end of the project. Some projects use earth-moving equipment for this process, and also to remove the top layer of earth above the upper level of archaeological features, but many do not and this back-breaking labour has to be done by hand.

Once the uppermost archaeological features are visible this first 'surface' will be carefully cleaned to reveal its key features and the slow process of archaeological excavation will begin:

recording (using pro forma recording sheets, notes, diagrams, sketches and photographs), then 'cleaning back down' in small increments. This process involves removing loose earth by hand using trowels, brushes and scoops to shift the earth first into buckets and then into wheelbarrows for storage. In many countries all this loose earth is sieved, to capture small finds and organic materials like seeds.

As time goes by and the excavation becomes deeper, there will also be additional surveying of prominent features such as walls, as well as recording of the relative heights of different features across the site and the stratigraphy of the trenches. Individual finds may be discovered that require careful measurement and further surveying before being removed. Larger features such as burials may also be uncovered and require specialised study. Any bones identified will be especially closely recorded, particularly partial or full skeletons.

Over the subsequent days, weeks or even months of an excavation this basic process of slow and careful recording and recovery will continue. Visitors to archaeological sites who are unfamiliar with the process are sometimes shocked at the slow speed of excavation. But there is an order to the process, a routine of precise steps of recording, measurement and survey. In the site office, the project director and his or her assistants will collate all the written notes, diagrams, photos and survey data, to build up a three-dimensional understanding of the site. They will use this data to adapt their thinking about the ongoing excavation and communicate those plans to the site staff. Projects usually have a daily, sometimes twice-daily, briefing to outline plans and changes to plans. There may be visits from colleagues, including local-government archaeologists involved in managing the archaeology of the surrounding area, who can contribute additional understanding of the site as it is excavated based on their knowledge of similar sites.

Eventually, the excavation will draw to an end; perhaps just for that season (some archaeologists have returned to the same site every summer for many years, and in some cases decades), or perhaps for ever. Some projects, undertaken in relation to activities such as the construction of new buildings or roads, will take place over a short time and once only, and the archaeological site will subsequently be destroyed or buried by the development. In such cases, the laborious process of data collection is all the more essential, as the entire site will be gone forever and only the records of the excavation left to interpret it.

And no matter what the project, a final closing down of the site will occur, removing all the records and equipment. On some sites this includes the final task of replacing all the earth removed and reburying the site. Only then can the third and final stage of an excavation begin.

Post-excavation

The post-excavation stage of archaeological investigation is the one most often overlooked by (some) archaeologists and the public; it is also often the most expensive in terms of time, money and resources. A general rule of thumb is that for every day in the field at least one and a half days of post-excavation will be needed, and frequently much more. In some cases it has taken decades to complete post-excavation work for projects which themselves lasted years; up to a decade in certain instances. This third stage, above all others, also makes clear whether or not the initial project design was well thought out.

A good design will have appropriately anticipated the post-excavation needs of the project and provided the necessary time, staff and resources to ensure that the outcome is a well-understood and archived project. A bad project design will do none of these things and will result in lost data, wasted time and money and, worst of all, a damaged or destroyed archaeological site that cannot be understood from the partial data that result. Our full understanding of hundreds of archaeological sites has been lost over the years because of failures either of project design and/or post-excavation work. Good projects, with well-run post-excavation work, result in a wonderful array of data, in a variety of formats, which can be studied and enjoyed by future generations.

Post-excavation comes down to five interrelated activities: management, assessment, analysis, preservation and dissemination. Taking these in order, management means managing (sometimes referred to as curating) all the records, photos, objects and files created during the project, ensuring that they are cross-referenced and indexed and stored somewhere secure and stable where they can be reviewed in the future. Management leads on to the second stage: assessment. This entails reviewing the different materials and types of data produced by the project, including artefacts, chronological (dating) and spatial data, and considering them in relation to other data (site records, photos, etc.) and to one another, building up a three-dimensional understanding of the site.

From assessment follows the detailed scientific analysis of the artefacts and ecofacts recovered, to glean more specific data about, for example, the ecology of a site, the type (and so the source) of the clay that any pottery discovered was made from, the specific sources of metal objects found on-site, and so on. Analysis includes examining evidence of chronometrically datable materials using radiocarbon dating or similar techniques, as well as evidence of links between communities, and where particular materials were sourced or traded from. Such scientific analyses require highly-trained staff and equipment costing hundreds of thousands or millions of pounds.

In turn, analysis leads to preservation, preparing specific artefacts for long-term storage in archives, or in some cases for museum display. The first stage is the stabilisation of materials immediately upon their recovery, carefully cleaning and drying the objects, removing loose dirt and making a record of their basic characteristics. The second stage is the longer-term conservation of the objects, any additional cleaning and in some cases repair (for example, filling in cracks in a fragile pot) to ensure that the condition of the objects will remain stable. This can include extensive scientific analysis, ranging from X-raying an object, to see if there is anything buried within it, to gently drying a wet object under controlled conditions.

The final stage, for some objects, is preparing them for public display. Only a tiny percentage of archaeological materials recovered ever end up on formal museum display; most are destined for archives, where researchers and the public can visit them as needed. The few objects put on formal display might need additional preparation to make them as stable as possible (for instance, creating an internal supporting framework within a large pot). They might also need a special stand made, to support their weight properly, or a special display case built to maintain very constant light, temperature or moisture levels. They will certainly need a carefully written description for the display case's information board or museum guidebook.

The last post-excavation process – engagement – *should* have been taking place throughout the project, from the minute the initial project design was discussed, during any fieldwork, to long after the end of the project. In the modern world, with the Internet, this means in part using different forms of dissemination of information: at the very least an accessible, interesting and regularly updated web page, perhaps including sound and video recordings. It also includes formal publications, from specialist reports for dedicated academic journals, to heavyweight academic books, to more accessible books written in non-academic language. An array of grey literature, reports that are unpublished but made available online or in archives, might be produced. Dissemination might also involve filming or recording for television and radio. But true engagement is more than just one-way dissemination of information: engagement means including as wide a range of people as possible in a project, using diverse methods. Engagement involves two-way dialogue, through a full array of public archaeology events: site visits and tours, lectures and seminars and, crucially, opportunities for community involvement. These often extend to public involvement in the post-excavation process, such as community involvement in the assessment and analysis of data.

The role of theory

As the Anglo-American archaeologist Matthew Johnson explains in his 2010 book *Archaeological Theory: An Introduction*, 'what makes us archaeologists as opposed to mindless collectors of old junk is the set of rules we use to translate these facts into meaningful accounts of the past'. These rules of higher-level examination and explanation of the past are usually referred to as 'theory'. Theory is as central to practical archaeology as any other tool. The only difference is that theory is a tool for thinking rather than doing, although those thoughts often translate into later actions. Theory puts archaeology in a cultural context and this context changes all the time, depending on who you are and who you ask, the asking of which is itself a theoretical act.

This sounds like a self-justifying cycle but such a statement is underlain by a fact worth considering: *people are interested in the past and think that the past is important for all sorts of different reasons.* These different reasons are as worth thinking about as the past itself. People have in the past thought that 'their' past was important for very different reasons and the same is true today. Different people, cultures and societies have very different takes on the past. Admitting to our own biases and preconceptions, and trying as much as we can to overcome them, is central to the practice of archaeology. This is something that all scientists, no matter what their subject, do and is part of the broader ethical responsibility of research.

This filters down to a series of real actions on the ground. It means, for example, publishing data in a timely, readable manner; it means including in your publications information about what went wrong as well as what went right in the project; it means making clear things such as how the research was funded and what impact, if any, that funding had on the decisions made and the outcomes that resulted. It means making your basic data available for others to study in order that they might test, and possibly challenge or refute, your hypotheses and conclusions. It means, ultimately, acting in a civilised manner, being a systematic and thoughtful researcher who has respect for him or herself and for others.

Related to this is the fact that not all interpretations of the past are equal. There are good, bad and indifferent interpretations, and we need to distinguish between them, as well as decide what criteria mark out the good from the bad. Theory helps us to do this. Some interpretations are bad because they are mistaken: the wrong type of data or not enough data were considered, a mistaken hypothesis was formulated or a mistake made in a scientific analysis. By learning about, and from, such mistakes, better hypotheses can be created and better interpretations will result. But other interpretations, where someone has chosen to ignore some data or prioritise others, are wilfully wrong.

To help explain the practical role of theory in archaeology, consider some of the theory-related circumstances of the series of Mesolithic burials in the Skateholm area of Sweden, which have been developed since the late 2000s. Occupied between 6000–400 BCE, Skateholm consists of a series of Late Mesolithic settlements around a brackish lagoon on the coast of the Scania region of southern Sweden. The people who lived at Skateholm were hunter-fishers who exploited the lagoon's marine resources, but the size and complexity of their cemetery area suggest that it was used for a broader ritual purpose, as a distinct burial place for special individuals.

The special status of some burials at Skateholm is indicated by the position of those buried in the cemetery and also the unequal distribution of grave goods. At Skateholm, elderly men and young women received the largest quantity of grave goods. Some burials contained unusual grave goods. One young man was buried with several pairs of red deer antlers placed above his legs; in another grave, a dog was buried on its own, together with an antler headdress and three flint blades. In addition, while most of the bodies were conventionally placed, lying on their backs with their limbs extended, a small number were buried sitting up, lying down or crouching, while others were cremated.

The Skateholm burials have been intensively analysed by a series of archaeologists since 1979, but in the late 1990s and early 2000s a number of different archaeologists reassessed many of the burials, exploring the ritual dimensions of the mortuary practices at Skateholm in comparison to other cemetery sites in Scandinavia. For example, the archaeologist Fredrik Fahlander suggested that a distinction can be made between 'non-aggressive' and 'aggressive' manipulations of the graves and bodies. Comparing the data from Skateholm with data from the Middle Neolithic site of Ajvide on the island of Gotland, he proposed that aggressive manipulations are generally the result of social stress during periods of hybridisation between different groups and traditions; that is, people embodied their wider social worries and problems in their burial practices, adapting them to reflect their contemporary concerns.

In contrast, the archaeologist Liv Nilsson Stutz compared the mortuary practices at Skateholm with those at Vedbaeck-Bøgebakken in eastern Denmark. Using a combination of methods and theories that focus on the ritual practices as action, she proposed an alternative approach to the burials to Fahlander, giving special attention to the ritual practices of handling the bodies of the dead and different dimensions of rites of passage at death. The key was not the burial itself, as Fahlander proposed, but rather the activities surrounding the burial process; that is, Fahlander's analyses place the social emphasis on the burials having special social meaning (especially how burial types and inclusions changed over time), whereas Stutz's analyses place the social emphasis on the *process* of burial having meaning (how people went about preparing for and undertaking a burial). This application of different philosophical approaches to the same data set is archaeological theory in action. The wider understanding of societies, both ancient and modern, which results from such contrasting analyses is the added value of archaeological theory, the justification for taking the time to undertake the work.

3

The archaeology
of objects

Think about all the different objects you have in your possession. Now consider which might survive a hundred, a thousand or ten thousand years from now. Then think about understanding these objects without the benefit of the understanding of your own life and world, which archaeologists refer to as 'social context'. If you discovered your mobile phone a thousand years from now, would you even understand what a mobile phone was, or what its function was, let alone its subtle social symbolism and what it implied about your age, gender, and social or economic status? Think also about how you would manufacture (or at least might manufacture), or gain through trade or exchange, some of the objects you possess.

Constructing objects from 'natural' materials, manipulating the environment in this way, lies at the heart of archaeological understanding of surviving objects and what they tell us about past social complexity and organisation. All these issues, and more, are the types of questions that archaeologists deal with in relation to the objects that they discover, from big to small, ancient to modern. The pursuit of intangible information and knowledge through the examination of objects lies at the heart of archaeological enquiry. This includes examining the interrelationships between discoveries, mapping the densities and statistically meaningful quantities of objects found on archaeological sites and between different sites, over both short and long distances.

A starting point for any discussion of objects in archaeology is the consideration of how such objects influence the wider landscape; that is, when an object becomes not a simple object but a feature. Across Australia you will find 'scarred' or 'canoe' trees; trees whose bark has been removed, often repeatedly and over several generations, for the creation of bark canoes, containers and shields. Such trees are both natural parts of the landscape and also cultural objects in their own right, through their adaptation by humans. They have been altered by the Indigenous population for prosaic, practical reasons, to gather bark for reuse, but they also serve a broader symbolic function for their communities. Some scarred trees have a ceremonial function; their scarring is decorative, not functional. Other trees function as landscape markers, wayfaring and/or gathering points for communities. These trees are an example of how an object can be both a single, stand-alone feature and part of a wider landscape. Many other examples of such landscape objects exist around the world, for example, prehistoric rock art and standing stones, medieval stone and wooden crosses and, more recently, the crosses commemorating victims of the First World War.

Another question with respect to the analysis of scale in relation to objects is the issue of 'portability': can the object that you are studying be moved? Despite the popular perception that people moved around very little in the ancient world, in fact people – and objects – regularly travelled hundreds or even thousands of miles (see Chapter 6). An archaeologist cannot assume, therefore, that an object comes from the immediate vicinity of the spot where it was found. For the ancient world, the question of portability restricts study to relatively light objects, weighing up to a few tonnes, that could be carried by boat (the easiest way of carrying heavy loads), in a cart pulled by animals, or by people, either on their own, in groups or with the aid of animals. Portability is not a perfect measure of what makes an object. For example, many objects are made from numerous components, all of which are portable yet which can be put together to create a much larger and vastly more complicated object.

Clearly, even many non-portable objects are still single objects in their own right; they represent a distinct entity in and of themselves. Think of major buildings or monuments; even though they are very big, they are still objects. Single-object status relates to the important issue of how objects interact with one another, in both physical and cognitive landscapes. A small, portable, bead, for example, may have been used by humans for activities such as trade and exchange, and thus have come into contact with many other objects, places and landscapes via the people that used it. Tracking the patterns of movement of different materials is a key field of study for archaeology, since tracing ancient trade routes can tell us much about ancient political and cultural contacts and alliances. Visual representations of objects can also be carried, so you do not even have to have an original object for this process.

As an example, consider the modern financial system. First coins, then paper notes, now credit cards and, increasingly, simple credit transfers, have all represented money but they are increasingly divorced from the physical reality *of* money. Originally, objects such as coins were literally valuable pieces of precious metal, whose worth came from their physical weight and value. Coins could be melted down for their bullion value or buried, to be rediscovered by future archaeologists. Later, objects such as paper notes and cheques were used in lieu of coins but could still be exchanged in a bank, at least in theory, to claim credit from a physical reserve of precious metal. Now, formal physical reserves of precious metal are largely unnecessary and are maintained only by national banks and governments and a few private individuals.

How, why and where objects were made and used

The archaeological examination of how, why and where objects were made and used calls for the deployment of an array of scientific techniques to examine, often at the microscopic level, the materials that an object was constructed from and where those materials originated. This includes wood, stone, bone, ceramic, and so on, which can be traced to specific locations, thanks to distinctive characteristics in their microscopic make-up.

This process of examination also includes considering the evidence for an object's age, both by association (relative dating) and through scientific analysis (absolute dating). Such examination includes the study of use and reuse of objects, noting wear-marks and patterns. Many objects bear traces of the processes involved in every aspect of their 'use life', from the marks made during construction or manufacture, to the final act that led to their loss or discarding.

Thinking about making objects raises profound issues relating to our understanding of human cognition and development, of how humans first began to construct relatively simple objects made from one or two constituent parts and how, over millennia, we as a species moved on to make more and more complex objects from multiple different components.

Our use of the terms 'simple' and 'complex' should be extremely cautious: these are culturally relative terms. A stone axe manufactured in the Acheulean period (from about 1.65 million years ago to about a hundred thousand years ago) is made of one material, and is simple in comparison to many modern devices, even to a similar tool, such as a kitchen knife. But it is simple only in terms of its raw materials, not in the skills involved in its manufacture. Few people in the modern world could make either a similar stone axe or a kitchen knife. They would not know where to find the raw materials, nor would they know how to use other tools, such as stones of different density, to deftly turn the raw piece of stone into a finely-worked tool, or indeed where to find the hammer stones crucial to the tool's manufacture. Nor, finally, would they know how to handle the finished tool. These processes of manufacture are anything but simple, even for an ostensibly humble stone axe. Such processes are many times more complicated for objects made of multiple or composite materials. For example, alloys only function correctly when specific types of metals are blended together in precise quantities at precise temperatures for precise lengths of time. Archaeologists, therefore, spend a lot of time and effort analysing the sources of materials.

Experimental archaeology (experimenting with ancient manufacturing techniques) plays a major role in understanding the manufacturing processes and uses of objects. Returning to the example of the stone axe, the use of this object seems obvious: it is a tool, an axe. But thinking more carefully, what does this really mean? An axe for cutting what, in what context? Felling whole trees, chopping off the branches of fallen trees or cutting the bones of the large animals that were hunted? How was the axe used? Was it attached to a shaft, to provide greater leverage? If so, how was that shaft constructed, of what materials and how were they processed? How was the axe attached to the shaft? Were there bindings made of plants, animal skin or something else? Assuming that the axe had a shaft and so approximated to our modern understanding of an axe, how was it handled? Was it used similarly to today, swung overhand or overarm, or in a totally different fashion? How was the axe kept sharp? Or was it simply used until it became blunt, then discarded? Finally, was the axe actually used as a practical tool, or was it a symbolic item, carefully manufactured to represent a social or cultural meaning, or perhaps to be offered as a gift?

These are the types of questions – to do with social complexity – that archaeologists ask of objects. Remember, this is but one example of one stone axe: many archaeological sites discover thousands of objects, some of great technological complexity and all of which have to be analysed in relationship to one another.

Trade and exchange

Studies of the place of objects in trade, exchange and reciprocity (mutual gift-giving) involve examining the movement of objects *between* peoples and thus the reasons for, as well as practicalities of, such movement.

In some cases the movement of objects may be small, relatively simple to understand and carried out over a short distance. A modern example would be one family member giving another family member a home-made cake for their birthday. But in antiquity many objects were moved across considerable distances and exchanged between groups for varied reasons, sometimes as purely practical items of trade and exchange (bartering one set of useful materials for another set of different but equally useful materials), at other times exchanged for esteem or recognition (for example, gifts of treaty to more powerful groups, either as a sign of submission or as a result of having lost a battle), or at others used as items of social bonding, ritualised gifts linking individuals, such as gifts at marriage or initiation ceremonies, or as acts of alliance between groups.

Other objects have been moved – the more appropriate word in this context is 'dispersed' – in the past as a consequence of theft, war or disasters such as famines or plagues. For example, objects were often intentionally buried for safekeeping but never recovered. Some objects were also intentionally buried and/or destroyed in deliberate symbolic acts associated with forms of ritual and religion, to venerate or appease a god. And, last but not least, objects both large and small, from a coat button snagged on a branch to an entire ship wrecked in a storm, were simply lost.

TRADE AND EXCHANGE IN THE ANCIENT AEGEAN

An influential example of ancient communication networks and supply chains that revolutionised our understanding of social complexity in the past is the obsidian trade in the prehistoric Aegean. Obsidian is a naturally-occurring volcanic glass that can be crafted into tools. Around twelve thousand years ago, the island of Melos in the Aegean was a noted source of obsidian, which was sent to the mainland of Greece. Discoveries of obsidian tools have been made throughout the region, particularly at Franchthi Cave in mainland Greece, which was excavated between 1967 and 1976 by a team led by the archaeologist Thomas Jacobsen. When these tools were examined and the composition of the obsidian analysed, it became clear that the majority of the stone came from one particular location, the island of Melos, which had *always* been an island, never connected to the mainland. The conclusion was clear: from the Upper Palaeolithic period a regular supply chain of obsidian had run from Melos to several other places. This supply chain needed both social networks and technologies: people quarrying the obsidian, people (perhaps the same, perhaps others) passing it on, boats to carry the obsidian to the mainland (although no watercraft survive from this time), crews for the boats and distributors on the mainland.

This is one of the earliest known examples of the supply chains that make the modern world what it is, politically, socially and economically. This type of supply chain is essentially the same system that brings us everything from bananas to motor cars: a social network that depends on communication, collaboration, and above all trust in the process of regular supply of a material meeting regular demand, at a mutually-agreed price (whether money, bartered goods or exchange), time and quality. Understanding, through archaeology, how such supply chains developed is a crucial part of our understanding of ancient activity.

A different example of the process of trade and exchange comes from a nearby location off the coast of modern-day Turkey: the Late Bronze Age shipwreck at Uluburun. Dating from the late fourteenth century BCE, this site was discovered in 1982 and excavated between 1984 and 1994 by a team from Texas A&M University. Thousands of objects were discovered on the wreck, including more than 350 raw copper ingots (probably from Cyprus) weighing over ten tonnes, 150 Canaanite-style jars with resin residues, made of clay that indicates an origin in Egypt, and about 175 glass ingots, again probably from Egypt. There was also a rich cargo of smaller items, including blackwood logs from Egypt, elephant ivory tusks, hippopotamus teeth (used in jewellery), ostrich shells from central Africa, Cypriot pottery and oil lamps, and mixed jewellery materials including Baltic amber, agate, carnelian, quartz, gold, faience and glass from both Egypt and Cana (the present-day Gaza Strip, Israel, West Bank and Lebanon). The Uluburun shipwreck yielded a cross-section of objects from around the eastern Mediterranean; it is of immense significance to archaeologists, both for the objects discovered and the analysis of their origins and manufacturing processes.

One of the richest shipwrecks ever discovered, the site has also given us a unique insight into Late Bronze Age trade and exchange in this region. From an analysis of the cargo, it appears that the vessel set sail from either Crete or Cyprus and worked its way anti-clockwise around the eastern Mediterranean, trading, exchanging and bartering at ports along the way. When it was wrecked off the south coast of Turkey it was probably on the final leg of its voyage, either heading home, perhaps to the islands of Rhodes or Crete, possibly further west into the Aegean or even, potentially, to mainland Greece or Italy. Its crew's loss was our gain, giving access to a microcosm of trade and exchange in this place and period.

The social context of objects

Examining the symbolism of objects involves considering the social context, value and meaning beyond their immediate physical use or monetary or barter value. This includes analysing how objects operate as evidence of non-physical decisions, of social complexity and organisation in the past.

Some objects have an immediately obvious practical value as a tool or weapon, or a monetary value as a precious piece of metal or a jewel. But even workaday objects can have hidden or higher symbolic meanings beyond their practical or monetary value. Some symbolism is very individual and private, known only to one person or a small number of people; the keepsakes such as a lock of hair or a favourite toy that are common to us all. If discovered by another individual, it is unlikely the symbolic value of such objects could ever be deduced from a simple analysis of their functional form and characteristics. Other objects have a symbolic function shared by larger social groups, whole communities or societies, such as objects associated with specific religions that bear symbolic motifs.

In different societies, many objects, especially more complex objects, had complex rituals associated with the different stages of their life, analogous to the stages of a human life, from construction or 'birth', through childhood and the period of transfer into adulthood associated with adolescence, through middle and older age, to 'death', the object's loss or disposal beyond reuse, be that real or symbolic. This final stage is the reason why archaeologists often find deliberately buried or abandoned materials that have come to the end of their lives and been subject to what amount to 'funerals' that ritually end the use life of an object.

'Artefact biographies' are a relatively new archaeological approach to such issues. This concept endeavours to better understand the information that can be extracted from an archaeological artefact in order to reconstruct its life history. Providing information on past technologies, technological innovation and the development of craft specialisations, such an understanding of the range of processes that underlie a single object is referred to by archaeologists as the *châine opératoire* (operational sequence), a methodological tool for analysing step by step the technical processes and social acts involved in the production, use and disposal of artefacts. Such information enables the investigation of the sources of raw materials, the technological choices and the spatial, economic and social factors that influenced past makers and users.

The Egyptologist Kathryn Piquette uses an excellent example of artefact biographies in her teaching at University College, London, taking the example of a small faience amulet of a frog. This amulet can be subjected to a range of analyses that identify the material and the technological features underlying its production. The identification of the material – faience – that the frog is made of leads to the study of the broader history of production of faience in ancient Egypt, as well as to an analysis of the amulet itself, in which specific scientific techniques can be applied. This more advanced level of examination helps characterise the composition of the raw materials used in the frog.

The artefact biography for the frog is a complex sequence reflecting the production of such amulets in the New Kingdom of Egypt (sixteenth to eleventh centuries BCE). Part of an organised and controlled system that involved gathering raw materials from a wide variety of sources within and beyond Egypt, the artefact biography also demonstrates extensive co-operation with other industries: using pottery-makers' clay for mould-making, firing the faience in their kilns, and sharing workshops, colouring oxides and materials with glass producers, and metal oxides and tools with metal workers.

Which objects survive?

The question of which objects survive in the archaeological record involves examining the processes underlying their survival. These processes include both *cultural* factors (both why people discarded certain objects and carefully preserved others and also the processes of the objects' loss or discarding, curation or preservation), and *natural* factors (the environmental conditions of an archaeological site, which can influence the rate and type of decay of objects. Similarly, the materials an object is made from affect survival rates. Hard, inorganic materials such as stone and ceramics survive, in general, much better than softer organic materials such as fabrics, skins and plant products.

The issue of which objects survive also raises the issue of caring about objects, in the past as well as in the present. One aspect of the archaeology of objects is the minute analyses of wear patterns, the subtle evidence of the use life of an object. This includes evidence of repair or maintenance (such as repeated sharpening of a blade), of accident (such as a tool with a broken tip that nevertheless remains in use), or of reuse (especially of discarded or broken materials). For example, in classical antiquity a common use for broken bits of pottery was as the modern equivalent of scratch pads, on which short notes, reminders and so on were either scratched or inked. Such analyses help reveal information about the objects' users, either individuals or groups, for example, when particular wear patterns indicate the user's handedness. Above all, evidence of use indicates people's levels of care and emotional investment in an object: whether an object was carefully maintained and prized, used heavily or lightly, casually discarded or abandoned after long use and repeated repair. This can include evidence of conspicuous consumption, of the deliberate discarding of objects, in which the apparent lack of concern regarding the loss of a valuable item is used to indicate wealth or status.

The question of the survival of objects also includes the analysis of the processes of manufacturing *multiple* objects of the same type and the related issue of consumerism and sustainability; of needing 'enough' objects and what 'enough' means for different communities and individuals. The modern world is not alone in its vast variations in the scale of ownership of material possessions within communities, let alone among different societies. The particular issue of mass-market consumerism fed by complicated manufacturing processes often located far from but linked to a society by equally complicated supply chains began, by and large, with the industrial revolutions of the eighteenth and early nineteenth centuries. These manufacturing processes were refined in the assembly-line systems of the later nineteenth and the twentieth centuries. None the less, before such sophisticated systems were in place, there was still manufacturing. The difference lies in the nature of the manufacturing, its processes and products.

In terms of processes, the analysis of materials and manufacturing entails the study of what are sometimes, rather unfairly, termed 'cottage' industries. This term belies the scale of these industries. Think, for example, of the amount of ironworking for a diverse array of purposes undertaken around the world for thousands of years by millions of unknown and unnamed blacksmiths, fed with their raw materials by similar legions of unknown miners. The commonness of variations of the name 'Smith' in Europe and European-populated locations indicates the vastness of this industrial activity. Although widely dispersed (pretty much every locality, even the very smallest, had its forge) rather than focused in specific locations, these cottage forges were still involved in manufacturing on a vast scale. Some ancient smiths regularly spent days or weeks producing one particular product; horseshoes or nails, for example. While many undoubtedly also undertook a variety of work, both manufacturing and repairing as needed, such specialisation was mass production by any standards. The same can be said for many other industries, from baking to pottery-making to basket-weaving.

The major difference between such craft production and later production-line processes is that individuals undertook these craft processes on occasion, as required. However, in other regards ancient industrial activity bears strong comparison to more modern manufacturing. For example, many ancient cities had distinct manufacturing zones, as in the modern world. These zones often had specific sub-zones, both where particular trades clustered for social cohesion and support (the origins of guilds and unions) but also because of environmental issues or needs, such as a trade needing a lot of water for its manufacturing process, or being particularly noisy, noxious or dangerous. Above all, until the Industrial Revolution, all manufacturing processes were to some extent bespoke: the hand of a particular worker would have been visible in small variations in each different item, even when thousands of nails, for example, were produced at a time. Only when the Industrial Revolution brought mechanisation and later computerisation, and production lines, did uniformity of production and product come into being, resulting in millions of identical objects.

Environmental impacts on survival

The starting point of the archaeology of environmental survival is the initial point of loss, disposal or deposition (immediate-term factors). The initial stage, loss, may be due to overwhelming environmental conditions, such as when we lose a set of keys during a winter storm, and the loss goes unnoticed until it is too late to do anything about it. The second stage is the first few hours, days and weeks after the loss (short-term factors). In this stage, the decay of organic objects will be particularly swift, due to bacterial, insect and animal attack, and decay. The third stage is the months and first few years after the loss (medium-term factors). Under the right circumstances, preservation of objects in this stage may be very good, for example if an organic object is rapidly buried and thus protected from the elements. The fourth stage is the tens, hundreds and thousands of years after this (long-term factors). Depending on the speed of loss/disposal/deposition, the question becomes one of environmental extremes, all of which interact:

- *Acidic versus alkaline*: extremes of both in the environment can, depending on circumstances, be either very good or very bad for the survival of objects. For example, the very acidic, sandy soil of the Sutton Hoo ship burial in Suffolk, UK, almost entirely destroyed the timber hull of the main ship burial but left the metal grave goods relatively well preserved, including an array of weapons, armour, tools and cooking equipment, most famously the richly-decorated helmet with the face of a moustached man.

- *Wet versus dry*: both extremes can be very good for survival but the middle ground can be disastrous. In some circumstances, underwater sites can lead to perhaps the most exceptional survival of materials seen on any archaeological site. Little Salt Spring in central Florida, USA, is a sinkhole full of fresh water that was used as a prehistoric burial site. The particular blend of aquatic conditions in the sinkhole (a low-oxygen environment and the presence of certain dissolved minerals) preserved prehistoric human body parts, including brain tissue. Similarly, very dry sites, both very hot deserts and very cold tundra, can preserve materials well, through desiccation or refrigeration. The former includes many examples from ancient Egypt, the latter prehistoric materials, including the remains of entire woolly mammoths, from places such as Arctic Russia and mountain sites in the High Andes of South America.
- *Hot versus cold*: again, both extremes can be good for survival but the middle ground not so, particularly in relation to other conditions. Survival of materials from archaeological sites in the tropics, or along or close to the equator, where the climate is hot and damp, can be very mixed. This is in contrast to the extremes of the high Arctic and Antarctic, where the cold, dry air acts as a giant refrigerator, and with the deserts of the world, where the hot, dry air desiccates materials.

Two other related factors determine the survival of materials on an archaeological site. First, there are external – mostly human – impacts. If left alone by humans (and wild animals that dig and burrow), archaeological sites become stable, sealed units, whose stability assists their survival. But the second humans or animals expose buried materials, a ticking clock of decay begins, opening the objects to bacteriological or other attack, unless controlled by conservation. Second are the related issues of ground density and depth of burial; materials buried or absorbed into relatively soft, dense, deep surroundings tend to survive better than those in shallower, loose or large-grained media. These factors influence an object's likelihood of decaying, due to the levels of surrounding oxygen. In ideal circumstances an object will be buried or rapidly absorbed into a fine-grained matrix (fine silts, clays or the like). Particularly if the environment is cold, this can lead to very low oxygen (anaerobic) conditions around the object, which inhibits decay.

As an example, consider the case of the Tudor warship *Mary Rose*, which sank in 1545 off Portsmouth on the south coast of the UK. The recovered wreck is now on display in a purpose-built museum in the city. This is one of the most important archaeological sites in the world for the study of the survival of organic remains and the members of the team that worked on the site have become recognised as global experts on the conservation and display of such objects. The seabed in the area where the *Mary Rose* sank is primarily comprised of fine-grained silt and the water is relatively cold. The site of the wreck is also in fairly shallow, sheltered water. These environmental factors make the wreck site an excellent case study in the archaeology of preservation and decay in relation to site formation. The precise circumstances of the loss of the *Mary Rose* are not fully understood, but on sinking, the vessel became embedded in the seabed on its starboard (right-hand) side. Over the years, different densities of sediment worked their way into every corner of the wreck. The finest-grained sediments worked their way into the deepest recesses of the hull, to places which even the hungriest of marine scavengers could not reach. Larger sediments built up above these finer layers, creating layers of preservation. Meanwhile, as time went by, the exposed port (left-hand) side of the hull began to collapse in on itself. As the sediment built up inside the right-hand side of the hull and the left-hand side of the hull collapsed on top, the site began to stabilise, reaching a point of environmental equilibrium. Gradually, the dense sediments completely buried the vessel, and there it remained until it was rediscovered in 1971.

The excavation of the *Mary Rose* in the mid 1970s and early 1980s (culminating in its recovery in 1982) demonstrated how important the process of burial and collapse was in preserving many materials. Normally, almost all organic materials are lost on archaeological sites, due to biological and bacteriological decay. But in the case of the *Mary Rose*, the rapid burial of the ship in the cold, dark, muddy seabed meant that many objects were enveloped in a low-oxygen environment perfect for the preservation of organic materials of all kinds. Over years of painstaking excavation, archaeologists made many amazing discoveries of unique materials that do not normally survive. One of the most emotive of these discoveries was a wooden chest full of medicines, creams and ointments. Analysis of these medicines has given us an insight into the types of illnesses and wounds anticipated on board a ship of this period, from simple cuts and bruises, to burns from the newly-developed artillery that was carried on board, by way of syphilis from the crew's 'extracurricular' activities (the 'cure' for which involved injecting medicines, including mercury, into a very intimate male location). Some of these medicines still had the fingerprints of the last user embedded in them. Other discoveries included an amazing array of Tudor clothes and weapons, including boxes of bows and arrows ready for use. Numerous personal possessions of the crew were also discovered, from simple keepsakes to board games and musical instruments. Overall, the site offers a cross-section of Tudor life, all thanks to the unique circumstances of the loss and preservation of the starboard side of the hull.

Beyond their impact on the materials available for archaeologists to study, the conditions of preservation have practical issues as regards the immediate first aid and post-excavation stabilisation, conservation and display of objects. The moment that buried materials are exposed, the objects are open to renewed cycles of decay, unless conserved.

Immediately on discovery, this conservation involves first aid; stabilising the objects so that they do not decay further, including packing them for transport to a laboratory or other conservation facility. For major discoveries, weeks of planning may go into deciding on the best means of recovery and movement of a single object, such as the construction of special cradles to minimise damage. Once in the laboratory, weeks, months or even years of further study and conservation will be needed to gain the maximum amount of information about an object, as well as to ensure its long-term stability, whether in storage or on display.

The recovery and conservation of an object is merely one part of the wider picture of information that archaeologists build up around them. Before the initial discovery, the archaeologists involved will have made a survey of the object in relation to other features on the site as well as recording its immediately observable characteristics. They will have photographed and sketched the object and given it a unique reference number. All this data, together with additional data collected during recovery and conservation (for example, X-raying), ends up in electronic and paper archives and publications. Later, it will be collated in other archives and online, especially in the regional or national databases of objects maintained by local and national government.

A variety of interconnected cultural and natural factors influence the objects constructed by humans. What is left for archaeologists to find and decipher is a web of overlapping impacts on both the manufacture and recovery of such objects. Archaeologists try to work out which of these different factors had more or less sway on an object's manufacture, use and discarding. This analytical process comes down to seven major 'push' or 'pull' factors that can be examined for every object found. All these factors play a part in 'making' an object; it is simply a matter of interpreting the relative degree of influence in each case.

Materials

This question involves the analysis of the related issues of the materials that are available and manipulable. Some societies in the past lacked certain objects, because they did not have access to particular raw materials. This influenced what objects they could make; they either went without because they did not know better or else (an increasing trend of cultural sophistication) traded, exchanged and bartered for them. In extreme circumstances, communities might go to war to gain access to such materials or technologies.

This process of exchange, peaceful or not, can clearly have tremendous as well as disastrous consequences. As an example, witness the spread of tobacco addiction around the world after its discovery by Europeans on their arrival in the Americas. The Indigenous peoples had a long history of using tobacco before Europeans arrived in the sixteenth century but it took a peculiarly European commercial mindset to turn this into a global addiction and industry. Likewise, many ancient societies did not use the abundant metal ores that surrounded them simply because at that time they did not know that the rocks around them contained ores that they could exploit, nor how to extract the metal from those ores or work the metal that resulted.

Once societies became more sophisticated, the choice of materials available for use widened and so decisions on materials became less about practicalities and more about social choices and economic capacity (that is, what a person or their family could afford). In such circumstances, the choice of materials can be culturally indicative and decisions may not be made on common sense terms.

Environment

Environmental factors are a key area of study for archaeology. Indeed, for much of the history of archaeology, the environment was felt to be *the* key impact not only on objects but on *all* human behaviour.

Modern archaeological theory often contests the implication that the ultimate driving force of societies is their response or adaptation to different environments but it is still recognised as being highly significant. Work in this field includes studies of long-term climate cycles and regional environments (for example, global and continental level environmental variations). Medium-term changes to these cycles and environments, and more local variations, are also important, for example, regional and sub-regional variations determined by things such as altitude or proximity to the coastline. Short-term 'shock' changes to these cycles, and very locally specific environmental variations, are also visible; for example, the local fluctuations of land height and the proximity of rivers that lead to very specific and local environmental weather phenomena, such as fog building up at a particular place.

In terms of impacts on objects, this factor means two different things. First are the general practical issues of the influence of the environment on the clothes and shelter that people used, the tools they needed to manufacture, the materials they needed to gather or hunt, and so on. Second are the specific issues of objects being adapted to annual environmental cycles, which may be harsh or benign. A modern example of this type of environmental influence is the emergence of high-tech, lightweight, breathable waterproof fabric. Clothing made from such fabric has transformed the lives of millions of people, from commuters who want to travel to work without getting wet, to professionals whose lives depend on staying dry in extreme conditions.

An ancient example of this type of environmental influence is the famous 'ice-man', nicknamed Ötzi, whose body, dating from about 3300 BCE, was discovered in 1991 in the Alps, in the border region between Austria and Italy. Ötzi's clothes and equipment were designed for the harsh alpine environment and are exceptionally rare survivals that offer archaeologists a unique insight into an ancient man's adaptation to his environment. On top of a coat, Ötzi wore a cloak made of woven grass. Underneath the coat was a pair of leggings held up with a belt and, beneath them, a loincloth – precisely the type of clothing that modern climbers wear to build up insulating layers of trapped body heat. Ötzi also wore a bearskin cap with a leather chinstrap, again, warm and designed to stay on in high winds. His shoes were waterproof and wide, designed for walking across the snow; they were constructed using bearskin for the soles, deer hide for the top panels, and covered in netting made of tree bark. Soft grass went around the foot within the shoe, functioning like modern socks. It has been hypothesised that Ötzi's shoes were actually the upper part of snowshoes. According to this theory, other items, widely interpreted as being part of a backpack, were the wooden frame, netting and cover of a snowshoe.

Purpose

This is the issue of objects having one or more deliberate and/or accidental functions and thus of design compromises and modifications to reflect these sole or multiple uses.

A modern example is the different types of motor cars that exist. Some, such as Formula 1 motor-racing cars, are single-purpose, optimally designed to fulfil one task – high-speed track racing – but useless for others, being expensive to build, maintain and fill with fuel, difficult and dangerous to drive, and lacking practical facilities such as passenger seats or luggage space. These specialised vehicles contrast sharply with the majority of cars, which are exercises in compromise: speed versus load capacity, fuel efficiency versus looks, or cost versus comfort. The majority of purchasers compromise when they decide on a car, aiming for one that best balances their personal income and desires in terms of being relatively fast, efficient, spacious, good-looking, comfortable and expressing their desired or presumed status. Car manufacturers, meanwhile, go to great efforts to design vehicles that ever more closely match popular compromises, and advertisers expend similar effort in convincing us that 'this' car is 'the one'.

Similar variables of purpose can be witnessed in many other objects in daily use, both large and small; the modern world is full of both useful and frankly pointless objects. Some objects were designed with one purpose in mind but turn out to have accidental and often positive by-products. For example, many medicines were designed to meet one medical purpose but have turned out to have other uses, both legal and illegal. Similarly, the fast-acting adhesive, cyanoacrylate (superglue), originally developed as part of experiments to construct better gunsights during the Second World War, was developed as an industrial and household glue in the 1950s. It has even been modified for use as an emergency wound-sealer by the military and paramedics.

An ancient example is the different types of swords used in medieval and early modern Europe. Tenth- and eleventh-century swords were relatively short, broad weapons, sturdy and ideal for the close-quarter combat of that period. They were also, almost without exception, undecorated. In the fourteenth and fifteenth centuries, as time went by and sword technologies developed, especially due to experiments with different types of iron, swords became finer and longer. This gave their users a longer reach in combat but the swords were at risk of breaking, especially at their tips (this is the source of the term 'foible' for a flaw or shortcoming in character: a foible is the weak point between the middle and tip of a blade.) Technological change was accompanied by social change both in tactics on the battlefield and behaviour off the battlefield. While swords remained a military weapon, they became more and more common as a form of social display in civilian life; people wore them to show off. This social function accelerated the existing emphasis on length and also brought in increasingly ornate levels of decoration. First the hilt, then the scabbard and eventually even the blade of many swords began to be decorated. None of these changes did anything to improve swords' strength and usefulness; some actually disadvantaged the user by unbalancing the sword. By the sixteenth century, the situation had become so extreme that another term still in popular use had emerged: the 'swashbuckler'. This refers to a certain type of rough, noisy and boastful swordsman and relates to the use of a side-sword together with a 'buckler', a small shield designed to be used in single combat to deflect an opponent's sword. Wearing the sword on a belt, with the buckler alongside it, led to much noise: 'swashing and making a noise on the buckler'.

While the sword still had a deadly function, its purpose had been considerably modified over several hundred years. Such changes are reflected in the archaeological discovery of weapons, in the analysis of non-archaeological survivals of swords and armour, in architecture and, through changes in language use, in the historical record.

Ideology

All objects experience some ideological impact on their design. In some cases this impact is minimal; in others, considerable. The question is the extent of ideological impact. Understanding the influence of ideology on objects is something that both archaeology and society in general often have difficulties in getting to grips with, since the impact can seem vague and unspecific.

Consider the array of styles and designs of ancient armour used in medieval Europe. The cheapest, poorest armour was made from inferior metal or from layers of stout leather interspersed with wood padding. At this level, there is no ideological role at work; simply a practical concern. But the higher up the social scale and cost of armour one explores, the more ideology can be seen in play. Very quickly, the threshold of investment in practical improvements – of the lightest, strongest, most comfortable and thus practical armour – is reached. The sensible decision would be to stop at this point. But ornate engraving, ostentatious additional metal flourishes and even feather plumes on helmets, are all seen on armour of this type. Such additions were entirely symbolic; they served to highlight the wearers' wealth and social status but could often hinder their wearer in battle, sometimes with disastrous results.

At the Battle of Agincourt in 1415, a smaller and technically less well-armed English army defeated a numerically larger French army, which mainly comprised mounted knights, due to a combination of environmental and ideological circumstances. A recent hypothesis is that the heavy mud of the battlefield site, which is low-lying and had endured weeks of heavy rain before the battle, meant the lightly-armoured English had far greater mobility, while the heavily-armoured French got stuck. The French also underestimated the influence of the English (in fact mostly Welsh) longbowmen, who fired thousands of armour-piercing arrows into the narrow battlefield, forcing the French knights into a tight pack. Thinned out by the volleys of arrows and with many of their horses slaughtered, the French knights' heavy, overly-ornate armour was a hindrance, not a help, in the face of the under-armoured English knights and their unarmoured bowmen.

There is often a fine balance between practical and ideological impacts on the design of any object. This is true in the past as much as in the present, and may be hard to discern, especially in relation to ancient technologies, where issues of social identity in relation to gender, age or social status all influence design.

Technology

Although similar in some ways to issues both of purpose and material, the issue of technology is distinct unto itself. It relates to the tools and technologies (and so to people's cognitive abilities)

available for the construction of objects, as influenced by materials and purposes. To return to the example of ancient metal
working, if 'material' means the physical availability of raw materials such as iron ore, then 'technology' means the physical as well
as the cognitive ability not just to recognise but also to extract
and *use* the ore; to have the tools, knowledge and initiative to
mine, process and refine iron ore and to take the iron and make
it into other objects.

The ultimate, awful modern example of such technological
issues is the proliferation of weapons of mass destruction, atomic
and chemical, that require not only specific raw materials for their
manufacture but also specific techniques, tools and technologies.
An ostensibly more prosaic example from antiquity is the issue
of the particular types of metal and timber used for shipbuilding. Vessels of the Viking Age, such as those found at Skuldelev
in Denmark, in 1962, demonstrate the shipbuilders' exceptional
sensitivity to the timber available, and have profoundly influenced
archaeologists' understanding of ancient technological ability.

These vessels are constructed of long, thin oak planks, metic-
ulously split from whole trees that were clearly carefully selected
for their length and purity, having few knots and bulges. The
planks were further split into halves, quarters, eighths, sixteenths
and even in some cases thirty-seconds; an extremely complicated
and time-consuming process that took great skill. The result was
planks with enormous longitudinal strength, since the processing technique followed rather than split the grain of the timber.
Thanks to such archaeological survival, modern-day experimental
archaeology undertaken at the Viking Ship Museum in Roskilde,
Denmark, has revealed much about the skills of timber selection,
working and vessel construction in these communities. Following
the grain of the wood by splitting takes more time and skill but
plays to the strength of the timbers; cutting and sawing them
would be easier, faster and cheaper but would result in weaker
planks. When fastened together using carefully-manufactured

iron nails, the result was long, narrow ships of tremendous natural strength that required limited internal support and framing. These vessels were strong and seaworthy because of that strength, but also flexible; their construction meant that the planks, and thus the whole vessel, flexed and moved with the sea without too many leaks.

Tradition

Tradition can be a tricky concept. Identifiable 'traditions' – of technology, crafts, music, design and architecture – clearly exist as tangible concepts, demonstrated through objects, places and even landscapes (for example, traditions of particular designs of park or garden). However, traditions are also analytical concepts used by archaeologists to help understand the past: theoretical models that help structure and clarify our analyses but which would not have been explicitly identified by the actual people who made the objects.

One example is medieval European ship technology, which is often modelled by archaeologists in four traditions – the keel, the cog, the hulc and the punt – on the basis of the physically different design characteristics that are visible and identifiable by archaeologists in the surviving remains of such boats. Keels, cogs, hulcs and punts were all vessels but each tradition required quite different skills and technologies for their construction and these were often used in very different circumstances.

What is intriguing to archaeologists is how these different traditions are due to different technological, ideological, environmental and other determining factors and also how they intermixed and influenced one another. The simultaneous existence of four different shipbuilding traditions in a relatively short period (roughly, the ninth to fourteenth centuries CE) has few parallels in global history. As time went by, these four traditions intermixed to such an extent that a new type of multi-purpose vessel – the 'carrack' – emerged that combined all the best characteristics of the four older traditions in one package. This new tradition was greater than the sum of its parts, being both technologically related to and yet superior to all the other traditions. This carrack was the forefather of the great warships of the age of sail in the seventeenth to nineteenth centuries, a type of vessel only superseded with the advent of steamships.

The concept of a model or tradition is thus extremely useful to help us understand technologies and their interactions and overlaps. Traditions are visible not only in archaeology but in supporting documentary evidence, where variations in types and shape of vessel are noted by contemporary observers. But for all this, if we could travel back in time and ask medieval shipbuilders what tradition they were building a vessel in they would most likely express confusion and surprise; their answer would probably be 'we're building it the way we always have done, like our fathers and grandfathers before us'.

Traditions, therefore, are something that clearly exist but which are best identified *after* an event, since they are often not visible to people at the time. For all that, traditions are clearly an important determining factor in the construction of an object, especially in the impact of subtle variations in the design, construction and use of different materials.

Economics

Economics is the issue of the cost/benefit analysis of objects on the one hand and of the affordability of objects on the other.

We might decide to spend more on some objects in our lives because we recognise that the slightly higher initial expense is worthwhile in terms of long-term savings, because a slightly more expensive object may be more durable or reliable. Consider, for example, certain types of electronics: an inexpensive model of smartphone may not last very long because it is cheaply manufactured and has poor quality components; a more expensive model calls for greater initial outlay but remains in use for longer.

Allied to this are the issues of risk and time: economic judgements of the levels of risk involved in a purchase (a cheaper electronic device that you worry might electrocute you compared to a more expensive one that you don't think will) and our willingness to barter time for money. For example, it may be more expensive to take a taxi rather than catch the bus but by taking that taxi we may free up time for other pursuits, including making more money to offset the greater expense.

In terms of affordability, however, there are many people in our own society, and even more globally, who can rarely afford to make such cost/benefit choices between similar objects. Their poverty forces them to decide between entirely different classes of objects, between objects and bare necessities such as food, or even whether an object should be bought/bartered/constructed at all. This was also true for many people in the past. Discussion of all these different push/pull factors, which can be examined for every object, is what the archaeologists Hodder and Hutson, in their 2003 edition of the book *Reading the Past*, termed 'contexts'. Numerous factors play a part in making an object; it is simply a matter of degrees of influence. The different contexts are constructed archaeologically: the same object may have very different meanings and values in different contexts. Archaeologists thus must consider a variety of perspectives in the complex and uncertain task of translating the meaning of past texts into contemporary language.

This is why archaeologists use so many different tools to analyse the past. Some tools are practical, such as different types of scientific dating, using scanning electron microscopes to understand the composition of an object, and so on. Other tools are theoretical, such as the use of traditions as models to understand the past. Together, these different tools and techniques combine to provide, under ideal circumstances, the artefacts' biographies and ultimately the *châines opératoires* that lie behind every discovery.

4

The archaeology
of places

Imagine your home as an archaeological site. In the previous chapter we considered the materials that could be discovered there; the single objects that, when brought together, make our homes personal and distinctive. This chapter broadens that perspective to consider the wider picture of the places where such objects are discovered and how bringing all these different objects together makes a place a place. The scale is still relatively small – essentially, individual buildings or closely related groups of buildings – but now we will consider questions of the interrelatedness of individual objects rather than simply objects themselves.

To think about the archaeology of places, consider the history of different cities around the world. Investigations of such historic cities are especially common in the USA, where urban archaeology has revealed much about the organic development and underlying structure of relatively modern (in archaeological terms) places such as New York and San Francisco. But comparisons can also be made with more exotic locations: the street patterns, tight runs of narrow houses and close proximity of accommodation and service industries in cities such as New York are little different from the layout of the historic centre of Sydney, Australia. These cities are both examples of how historical layouts influence modern street patterns and how archaeology can offer

THE SYDNEY ROCKS DISTRICT

Now a thriving inner-city district catering for tourists and locals alike, the 'Rocks' district of central Sydney has the longest continuous history of occupation in European Australian history. Archaeological excavations since the 1970s have gradually pieced together this history, supported by documentary evidence.

Before Europeans arrived in 1788, the Rocks area had a long history of use by its traditional owners, the Cadigal, part of the Darug Nation, whose country stretched across modern-day Sydney. The arrival of Europeans was disastrous to these groups: within three years of settlement, half of the Cadigal population died, in what is believed to have been a smallpox epidemic.

Early maps of the Rocks show no prison buildings: the convicts' punishment was transportation to Australia, not incarceration in it. The land itself acted as an outdoor gaol from which there was no escape. Convicts were housed in camps that they built for themselves; the first dwellings were simple huts fashioned from wood and brick. None the less, by 1802, only fourteen years after the formal arrival of Europeans, the visiting French official Charles Alexandre Lesueur drew a map of the Rocks that shows how decisions made in the earliest years of the colony left a permanent mark on the future shape of Sydney. The map shows huts, two windmills for grinding grain, storehouses, a wharf, a church and a military battery. No archaeological traces of these first settlements survive.

From 1810 there was a conscious push to transform the town from a penal colony into a city. Consequently, by the 1840s, approximately 35,000 people lived in the Rocks and convict transportation had ceased. At this point, archaeological evidence begins to play a part in our understanding of the development of the city. Excavations, used in conjunction with documentary evidence, show that the Rocks became established as the commercial hub of the growing city, with exports from New South Wales exceeding its imports. Surviving buildings and archaeological evidence reflect this transformation into a mercantile centre; by the 1870s, many of the wealthier residents had moved out of the area to more comfortable suburbs, to larger homes set amid gardens. In turn – as reflected in the archaeological record – the Rocks began to change, with many of the houses becoming neglected and overcrowded. Archaeological evidence shows this transition, from modest merchants' houses to more ostentatious and larger properties that were then subdivided into multiple-occupancy homes. Materials surviving from these different periods also reflect these changes; modest domestic objects at first, then more and more evidence of wealth in the types of objects, especially imported ceramics, as the area grew wealthier, followed by larger numbers of cheaper, mass-produced goods as the area declined.

Throughout the later nineteenth and the early to mid-twentieth century, the area was subject both to decline and attempts to improve it. After an outbreak of bubonic plague in 1900, plans were put in place to remodel slum areas of Sydney, a process that has continued, off and on, ever since. Major projects such as the construction of Sydney Harbour Bridge (after 1923) and the Cahill Expressway (after 1955) further changed the area, leading to the demolition of hundreds of houses. Redevelopment plans were revised in the 1960s and early 1970s. Only after 1975 were the remaining historic buildings retained and restored, initiating the modern urban renewal of the neighbourhood that continues to this day, a pattern mirrored in historic cities around the world.

Figure 4 Archaeologists at work in the historic Rocks district of Sydney (copyright and courtesy of Mary Casey and Martin Gibbs)

insights into past behaviour that documentary sources alone are incapable of providing.

Archaeologists ask many questions of individual places, especially regarding social complexity and dynamics. This means analysing how people live, work and die together in distinctive places and how they structure those places in accordance with broader cultural rules. Such rules are influenced by, and influence, broader structures of settlement types and hierarchies, with considerable variations in living and working conditions between rural, suburban and urban environments.

Social complexity and dynamics

In terms of the archaeological understanding of place, the analysis of social complexity and dynamics means considering how physical places determine, and are determined by, social structures and cultural mores, such as the fact that some cultures have shared toilets for men and women, while others have separate facilities. Such physical structure is most visible when examining disparities between distinctive settlement zones on the grounds of social markers such as age, gender, wealth or (most difficult of all to define) class. Analyses can also examine internal social structures and hierarchies within groups or families.

An example regularly used when teaching archaeology students is the study of the home. Working on the basis of the 1950s 'nuclear family' comprising two parents and two children, the home can rapidly be divided into distinct zones, some private (bedrooms), others shared among the family and invited public (bathrooms, living rooms), others fully public (the front entrance and drive). Some zones may also be differentiated by particular uses (for example, kitchen and bathroom), which may or may not have tags of gender, hierarchy or other status associated with them (for example, 'mother' associated with the kitchen and 'father' with the workshop).

In the modern world, in which housing types and social structures are much more diverse, this simple model is less and less recognisable for many people. However, the basic principle stands, even if the structure of the space is more complicated. Many modern city dwellers live in extremely intermixed spaces, partly because space constraints reduce the amount of private space available to make strict distinctions between uses, but also because changes in roles have led to the greater sharing of household chores. Consequently, spaces such as kitchens, which until fairly recently would have had distinct operational and gender differentiation, have become very blended. No longer the domain of women, with distinct spaces for cooking, cleaning and washing, the kitchens of many modern city dwellers are a mixed-gender space, and one in which all these activities and more occur alongside socialising.

This model of mixed use has far more in common with much older patterns of blended social space seen in prehistory, for example in Iron Age roundhouses, than with industrialised views of social space. One of the markers of modern industrialised society has been greater and greater division of space on the basis of function, privacy and gender. But even within modern environments a careful examination of the micro-zones of any home will reveal distinct patterns; for example, clothing kept in distinct places and usually separated by gender. Such structures are likely to exist in great variety among all the homes of any neighbourhood, even if subtle differentiation on the basis of age, gender mix, social class and relative income influences the internal layouts, furnishings and uses of a home.

Such differentiations are likely to increase markedly in the space of just a few minutes' walk between different neighbourhoods. In most large cities, in the past as well as the present, great differences in age, gender mix, social class and relative income can be witnessed close together. Ancient Rome, just like the modern city, had poor and mainly youthful neighbourhoods abutting wealthy and relatively older ones. Patterns such as these are regularly seen by archaeologists working on historic homes and settlements around the world, dating from prehistory to the present day.

The medieval Cistercian monasteries of upland England and Wales are one of the best environments in which to appreciate the differential social layout of space in the past. Locations such as Rievaulx and Fountains Abbeys in North Yorkshire and Tintern Abbey in South Wales are well-preserved examples of the thousands of monastic estates that once covered Europe. Walking around these atmospheric ruins today, the sense of grandeur is easy to appreciate but the controlled use of space on the basis of gender, age, seniority and role, as well as time of day, month and year, is much harder to understand. Archaeological excavations at a variety of sites have served to better demonstrate these sites' complex histories, with multiple phases of development and distinctive living and working environments for different groups and individuals determined by their social status. Nowhere else in the world has such a breadth of archaeological as well as historic evidence survived – let alone been brought together – as in these examples. Advances in environmental archaeology since the 1970s, especially the sampling of organic remains preserved in rubbish pits, drains, toilets and other waterlogged locations, have supplied new insights into the nature of life in such places. More recently, since the 1990s, these data have been joined by more and more advanced analyses of human remains, sampling the bones of the monks to learn about their diet and physiology.

Archaeology has offered insights into the ages and regional backgrounds of the monks and nuns. Many joined in their youth, but some in middle or even old age, and they came from a wide geographical area, reflecting the extent of travel among their communities. Studies have revealed marked variations in diet among different members of the same religious order, depending on their social background, the rich diet (particularly high in meat and fish) enjoyed by the most senior members of

Figure 5 Fountains Abbey, North Yorkshire, founded in 1132 CE; Britain's largest monastic ruin and most complete Cistercian abbey (copyright of the author)

many communities, and the diversity of sources and distances from which food was brought. Saltwater fish, for example, was often transported in large quantities over hundreds of miles. Archaeology has also demonstrated the extent of medical knowledge and the medical care lavished on some individuals, shown by the presence and use of herbs and other plants to provide oils, ointments, balms and other aids to healing.

Rural places

One of the hardest things to do in archaeology is to securely define a 'rural' place or, rather more specifically, a truly 'wild' place untouched by humans. Archaeologists study people and their influence on materials and places; the archaeological mindset, therefore, effectively denies the existence of any truly wild, untouched place. Rather, we see only variations in levels of human impact, some very small, such as in the depths of the ocean, others very great, such as ancient cities. What is clear is that in the past, around the world, from prehistory to the present, there were a lot of rural places, relatively dispersed settlements more or less focused on some form of agriculture, be it hunter-gatherer landscape management at one extreme, settled farming at the other, or somewhere in between. It is equally clear that rural should not be equated with unsophisticated; for many cultures in the past it was not as simple as rural = unsophisticated; urban = sophisticated. This has major implications for the movement of people, goods and above all ideas through cultures, landscapes and places. Rural places can include both high- and low-status environments, with aspects of all the different types of social relation and space dynamics.

An example of the complexity of rural archaeology comes from the Severn Estuary, which lies between south-west England and south Wales. This is one of the most famous prehistoric landscapes in the world, thanks to its unmatched record of both archaeological survival and investigation. The Severn Estuary lies at the head of the Bristol Channel and it is the largest estuarine system on the British west coast. The estuary is highly dynamic, with an extremely large tidal range of nearly 15 m, and is exposed to the prevailing winds. Its waters are notoriously turbid, with the amount of suspended mud varying with tidal and weather conditions. The estuary is fringed by extensive areas of reclaimed alluvium, known as the Levels, which form a distinctive landscape. This makes for a rich historic environment in which the thick coastal mud has preserved many archaeological sites. In addition to its archaeology, the Severn Estuary is ecologically one of the

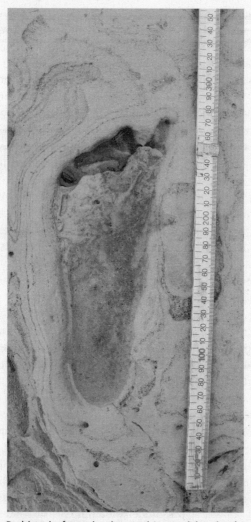

Figure 6 Prehistoric footprint impression surviving in the intertidal mud of the Severn Estuary in south-west Britain. The footprint dates from around 5500 BCE and is from a child of about ten years old (copyright and courtesy of Martin Bell).

most important and sensitive regions of north-west Europe, and is home to thousands of different species of plant and wildlife.

Since the early 1990s, archaeologists, including Martin Bell and Steven Rippon, have synthesised an array of evidence of how this landscape has evolved from prehistory to the present day. Archaeological, palaeo-environmental, documentary, cartographic, and place- and field-name evidence has been drawn together to examine the exploitation of this coastal area, showing that rather than being marginal, it was a rich and dynamic resource that was extensively exploited over the millennia by communities that enjoyed wide-ranging links with the wider world.

Hunter-gatherer communities left many traces on the late glacial and Mesolithic (early Holocene) land surface of the Severn Estuary, for example on the slopes of the former island of Goldcliff, where hearths, flints and food residues have been found. Some of these traces, buried by later estuarine sediments, have been found only because of modern coastal erosion. Later on, more sedentary prehistoric peoples exploited both the wetlands of the developing estuary and its adjoining dry land. Much evidence of their diverse activities – fishing, hunting, wild-fowling, reed-cutting and -burning, grazing, herding, trackway-building and peat-digging – has been unearthed from the silt and peat deposits beneath the Levels.

Eventually, Romano-British and medieval inhabitants followed. These communities made boats, used for transport in the estuary and the marshland creeks. Some, such as the Romano-Celtic Barland's Farm boat (built around 284–326 CE); the early medieval Magor Pill boat (of about 1164 CE); and the late medieval Newport ship (approximately 1445–66 CE), survive to this day.

This mix of environmental and archaeological data is the best-surviving, as well as best-understood, historic wetland community in north-west Europe and is potentially the most important in the world, with better time-depth and analysis than any other comparable site.

Suburban places

The archaeology of suburbs hardly seems a likely prospect from modern experience. 'Suburbia', to the modern mind, seems as far from the excitement of archaeology as it is possible to travel. But, in archaeological terms, 'suburbs' – the space between the rural and the urban – are fascinating places, increasingly studied in both the ancient and modern world.

The archaeology of suburbs involves studying the evidence of the reasons for suburbs, the driving forces behind their emergence and development, and what happens to them. Some suburbs are clearly planned and, indeed, in some cases the intention is equally clearly for such suburbs to *remain* suburbs; that is, to have a distinctive suburban character, usually a traditional patchwork of low-density housing and open space. As outlined in Robert Stern's 2013 book, *Paradise Planned: The Garden Suburb and the Modern City*, the various twentieth-century garden cities – planned suburban environments – that exist around the world are the prime examples of this. Towns such as Letchworth Garden City (begun in 1903) and Welwyn Garden City (begun in 1919), both in the UK, are two of the oldest examples of this phenomenon.

However, some suburbs are clearly organic and entrepreneurial, established on the fringes of existing urban environments to feed a particular demand of that town or city, to provide housing, industries or services that the city either cannot have or does not want within its boundaries. The development of such organic suburbs is fascinating for archaeologists, as these locations often have a very different social order and physical layout to the formal urban environment that they coexist with, an informal structure that is marked in their archaeology.

An example of the phenomenon of entrepreneurial suburbia is the Roman and medieval suburb of Southwark on the south bank of the Thames, now part of the modern city of London.

Southwark is one of the few intensively studied suburban environments anywhere in the world; it is also one that, in the Middle Ages, was central to the emergence of a global phenomenon: the Elizabethan theatre. It was in Southwark that William Shakespeare, Christopher 'Kit' Marlowe and contemporary playwrights and actors lived and worked in the mid to late sixteenth century, in a uniquely productive community.

As outlined in Cowan *et al.*'s 2008 book, *Roman Southwark: Settlement and Economy*, Southwark developed alongside the administrative and economic centre of London, which emerged on the north bank of the river around 43–50 CE. The two locations were connected first by ferries and later by a bridge. Clustered along the marshy southern shore of the Thames on a series of islands and areas of higher land, through the Middle Ages Southwark grew into a major service zone for its partner across the river. Many of the trades and services that the powers controlling London did not want within the city gravitated to Southwark. Some were unpleasant industries such as tanning and brewing, while others were socially ambiguous services, such as the theatre and prostitution. The technical landlord of and legal authority over much of this area, the Bishopric of Winchester, was happy for the suburb of Southwark to develop, growing rich from the tolls and taxes that could be levied on this zone of the counter-culture.

Although it is now largely buried beneath modern buildings, traces of the Roman and medieval settlement survive in the road layout and street names of the modern district and through a few surviving fragments of its structures. Archaeology has thus furnished the majority of information about the settlement. The piecemeal nature of such excavations, within the footprint of demolished or planned buildings, has none the less provided a good understanding of Southwark's major buildings, neighbourhoods and facilities. As discussed in Julian Bowsher's 2012 book, *Shakespeare's London Theatreland*, thanks to archaeological investigations in Southwark we have a unique insight into the development of theatres, the design of which both influenced, and were influenced by, the plays written to be performed there by writers such as William Shakespeare. The most famous example is the Rose Theatre, built around 1587, the remains of which were discovered and excavated in 1989. The series of archaeological sites of Elizabethan theatres in Southwark forms an internationally unique collection that has influenced how theatres have been built and plays performed around the world to this day.

Urban places

The archaeological study of urban environments has a surprisingly mixed and relatively young history considering the amount of time and effort now spent on it. Effectively, it was born from two movements that remain to some extent distinct. One origin is the study of abandoned urban environments, particularly in the Middle East, where urbanism originally emerged, but also in other historic urban areas such as South and Central America, where study has been taking place since the nineteenth century. The other origin is the study of occupied urban environments, particularly in the industrialised world, where the ancient remains of such cities are increasingly under threat from new development.

The former type of study remains predominantly research-driven, undertaken by academics from universities and museums in order to answer specific questions about ancient societies. Such archaeological fieldwork often analyses large areas of an ancient city at once and may take place over many years. The intention of such analyses is to get a very large slice in terms of both the physical and chronological space of the city. Two examples of such fieldwork are the ancient cities of Merv in Turkmenistan and Çatalhöyük in Turkey, where archaeological fieldwork has been taking place for decades.

The latter type of study, in contrast, remains predominantly rescue-driven, undertaken by archaeologists working on sites before they are destroyed or reburied by new buildings. Such archaeological fieldwork is often undertaken in very small sections of an ancient city – often just within the footprint of the new building that will cover the remains – and possibly over days or weeks, on a tight schedule. Such fieldwork is constantly under way in places such as London, New York or Mexico City (formerly Tenochtitlan), as these cities continue to grow and be redeveloped.

Irrespective of how they come to be studied, cities make for fascinating archaeology. They often reflect many layers of continuous settlement piled on top of one another, covering thousands of years of occupation. Cities also often show marked differences in social complexity and dynamics; that is, different types of high- or low-status, age- or gender-related structures or materials. Similarly, they often have marked differentiations between different zones of use – for example, housing, industry, leisure, ritual and other areas. To this can be added commonly high densities of remains, including (if the archaeologist is lucky) well-preserved organic materials in wet areas such as wells or former riverbanks.

THE ARCHAEOLOGY OF ANCIENT MERV

Merv was a major city in Central Asia, lying on the historic Silk Road that runs between the Middle East and China. Founded around the sixth century BCE, it flourished as an administrative, trading, military and religious centre for hundreds of years. Located near the present-day city of Mary in south-eastern Turkmenistan, several cities have existed on this site, which is significant for the interchange of culture and politics at a site of major strategic value.

There is a long history of archaeological exploration at the site. Merv was intermittently explored throughout the late nineteenth and early twentieth centuries, before a concentrated campaign of fieldwork during the mid-twentieth century. Most recently, the International Merv Project, a collaborative effort including archaeologists from over a dozen different countries, has been undertaking work since 1992. Archaeological investigations have been crucial to identifying the history and different stages of development of the city, as well as to understanding the nature of daily life, little of which can be understood from the documentary evidence alone, which is fragmentary at best.

Merv lies on one of the main arms of the ancient Silk Road. A broad delta of rich alluvial land created by the Murgab River, which flows northwards from Afghanistan, forms an oasis at the southern edge of the Karakum Desert. The ancient city developed at the heart of this oasis, close to the course of the main river channel.

Archaeological investigations have shown that Merv has an exceptionally complex history that comprises a succession of cities, dating from the fifth century BCE to the present day, which together once covered over a thousand hectares. The city began in the fifth century BCE as an administrative and trading centre. Little is known about this first city, as it lies 17 m below the modern-day ground surface. In the fourth century BCE the earlier city was converted into a citadel and a vast new walled city, Antiochia Margiana (today called Gyaur Kala), was laid out, eventually covering over 340 hectares. From around 250 BCE Merv developed as an administrative, military and trading centre, and archaeological finds from this period reflect that significance and the richness of its international connections. In the seventh century CE, the coming of Islam changed the urban landscape and conduct of daily life in Merv – again, a change reflected in the archaeology – with the city becoming a centre for Arab expansion when a self-contained walled town, Shaim Kala, was built outside the eastern gates of the existing city. Shaim Kala included an impressive mosque, the ruins of which survive to this day. By the eleventh century CE this mosque lay at the centre of the thriving city of Marv al-Shahijan ('Merv the Great', today called Sultan Kala). Archaeological investigations have revealed the complexity of this planned urban environment, which had a planned street system and water supply, and continued to expand and develop through the Seljuk period (the eleventh to early thirteenth centuries CE).

Finally, in the early thirteenth century CE, the city went into decline after a Mongol army sacked Merv in 1221. The townspeople were massacred and the town burnt to the ground and abandoned.

Isolated, remote and confined places

It is worth considering the archaeology of a few special types of place that do not fit into the categories discussed above. These places coexist with, and are based within, the social distinctions already outlined but they are very different in terms of their structures and physical layouts. These places include sites of confinement such as prisons and asylums for the mentally or physically sick or aged, sites of defence or offence such as castles and forts and sites of specific function, particularly industries or services that might need to be set apart from society because what they do is unpleasant or dangerous, such as butchery, tanning, iron-working or the manufacture of munitions. Other sites of this type fulfil a specific role in an environmentally-determined position, such as lighthouses or signal stations. There are also sites of ritual and religion; the locations of some monasteries, nunneries and hermitages were chosen specifically for their isolation or environmentally harsh conditions. Some sites, such as ships and boats, may even be capable of moving from place to place, and so come into contact with mainstream society at certain times while being impossibly remote at others.

Archaeologically, such locations' distinctive roles often highlight or exaggerate physical distinctions in terms of status, age or gender. Monasteries, for example, usually contain only men undertaking specific tasks in a highly ordered and repetitive manner within a distinctive, confined and strictly demarcated layout. Prisons are very similar. Ships have an even more constrained physical layout, in which space is at a premium and hierarchies of space use and location are very visible. But archaeology has to be very careful in undertaking such analyses. Nunneries have a very similar layout and material culture to monasteries but house women not men. The question is: what if anything differentiates a female from a male population in a religious location?

The easiest way to think about the archaeology of a particular place is to think about its defining characteristics, and few places have more distinctive defining characteristics than a prison. Thanks to countless shows and books, everyone has a mental image of a prison, usually unrelentingly grim. A prison is the ultimate exercise in proscription and the definition of a marked physical and *mental* place and space, set distinct from, while existing within, broader society. The internal physical layout, and so institutional social functioning, of different types of prisons can be carefully studied by archaeologists and anthropologists to pick up traces of their former occupants. Prisons offer insights into a society's attitudes towards different groups, such as the debate between the relative influences of nature and nurture in shaping people's behaviours, or whether criminals are made or born and thus how they should be punished or rehabilitated. From such starkly-defined places archaeologists learn a lot about less well-defined places and spaces, since the physical characteristics of prisons are a useful prompt for archaeological thinking.

The traditional image of a prison is that of nineteenth-century municipal prisons: serried rows of individual cells in grey stone buildings, with central communal spaces and an exercise yard, all surrounded by high walls. Modern versions may be drab, concrete-block buildings surrounded by razor wire. But other prisons take different forms: open prisons, for low-risk inmates, look very different and may at first glance not be thought to be a prison at all. In comparison, in the eighteenth and nineteenth centuries, old ships were often used as floating 'prison hulks'. Both are very different physical spaces from the traditional prison.

Prisoner-of-war, labour and concentration camps conjure up a very different mental image – of rows of identical wooden huts and bare open spaces surrounded by razor wire and machine-gun towers – from municipal prisons. But this is merely one form of such camps. Another type, the Arctic labour camps of Soviet Russia, bear comparison to the nineteenth-century labour camps built by Imperial Britain in colonies such as Australia. These often had no walls or other formal barriers to escape, but escaping from such physically remote locations was simply impossible and would only have resulted in a lingering death in the wilderness.

Two archaeologists working today have identified intriguing aspects of prisons that leave distinctive physical traces. Eleanor Casella, of the University of Manchester, has undertaken a series of studies of nineteenth- and twentieth-century prisons in the United States and Australia, which she described in her 2007 book, *The Archaeology of Institutional Confinement*. Her careful analysis of surviving materials from female prisoners reveals a wealth of data about the daily life of the inmates and the subtle ways in which they subverted formal authority, for example, using buttons as forms of internal prison currency. Meanwhile, the archaeologist Laura McAtackney, of University College Dublin, has, since the mid-2000s, examined a more recent prison site, Long Kesh / Maze prison in Northern Ireland, used to detain political prisoners – from both sides of the political spectrum – during the 'Troubles' of the 1960s to 1990s. The site is still largely in existence but undergoing redevelopment. The question is what, if anything, should be preserved of the prison as a physical reminder and memorial? With strong emotions on all sides and most of the former prisoners still alive, this archaeological analysis is as fascinating as it is difficult. It involves the physical study and preservation by record of the site through photographs, drawings and other documents, as well as oral histories of the site taken from former prisoners, guards and local people. This leads to the intermixing of archaeology and anthropology and the active participation of – and sometimes dispute within – the local community.

Archaeologists are particularly interested in analyses of the details of people's immediate environment. This is the study of what the surviving material culture and the spatial dynamics of different materials say about the places where we live, work and relax, and what these say about past social relations and dynamics. Archaeologists search for variations and especially interrelationships of evidence to do with scale and intensity in relation to some of the following:

Home

This word immediately raises the question of what we mean by a 'home'. In the modern industrialised world it conjures up images of a fixed, defined, distinctive, and above all private, social space occupied by a single or extended family, in which the primary (but often not exclusive) focus is a living rather than a working space. Additional signifiers of 'home' in the industrialised world are its distinctive subdivisions (different places for sleeping, eating, cooking, bathing and relaxing) and the distinctive types of electronic or other consumer goods found in those subdivisions; for example, few people would store a food blender in their bathroom or an electric toothbrush in their living room.

However, comparison with other present-day societies around the world, let alone with ancient societies, demonstrates how culturally subjective and also very new such images of home are. The philosopher Pierre Bourdieu studied the layout of different families' houses in the late 1960s, as part of his ethnographic research among the Kabyle Berbers of Algeria. Bourdieu placed particular emphasis on gender in understanding the spatial symbolism of the Berber house; something that more recent scholars have questioned, exploring other motivations such as kinship relations, status and the context of actions. But even allowing for such critiques, Bourdieu's work demonstrates how complex the spaces in which we live are, in their symbolic associations, the everyday fluidity of their various functions, and their cultural meanings, social configurations and spatial interpretations.

Within living memory, the 'homes' of 1930s Britain, the United States or Australia were dramatically different places to today's, particularly in terms of elements such as the provision of kitchen and bathroom facilities, gender roles and especially the presence and use of electronic consumer goods. Meanwhile, a comparison of modern homes in the industrialised world with those of large sections of the industrialising world reveals vast variations: far less private space and far more cross-family social interaction, far less subdivision of spaces, far fewer material goods to signify these separate spaces, and far more 'mixed' uses of spaces, in which a home can also be a workplace.

There are also many communities around the world for whom the very concept of a fixed, sedentary home is anathema: to the many different types of traveller communities, home is a far smaller, moving, space but one that still has extensive and subtle patterns of use and social structure. Indeed, for the majority of human history, sedentism (permanent settlement in one place) was not the norm. Through most of prehistory, small groups and entire communities travelled for a variety of reasons, particularly as hunter-gatherer communities. Only with the relatively modern rise of agriculture in central Asia, from approximately 7000 BCE, did humans begin to settle, at first forming small communities and eventually villages, towns and cities.

LIFE IN AN IRON AGE ROUNDHOUSE

The roundhouse is a type of building of a circular plan, with walls made either of stone or of wooden posts joined by wattle-and-daub panels, topped by a conical thatched roof. Roundhouses ranged in size from less than 5 m in diameter to more than 15 m. They were particularly common dwellings during the Iron Age in Britain (around 800 BCE to 100 CE). Archaeological sites with traces of these buildings abound across the British Isles, although the evidence is usually limited to post and stake holes, remains of burned hearths, collapsed oven remains and perhaps a scatter of pottery shards.

Although a large and ostensibly open space of shared use, the interior of a roundhouse would have had a clear differentiation of space on the basis of different functions. The fire was literally and metaphorically at the heart of the roundhouse. Constantly burning throughout the year, it provided the main source of light, kept people warm and dry and was where food was cooked and water heated. Smoke from the fire was used to preserve meat, hanging in the rafters above the fire, and also kept down pests and other vermin. There was no chimney or hole in the top of the roundhouse to let the smoke out; that would risk creating an updraught that could bring sparks into the roof thatch and burn the building down. Consequently, the interior of the roundhouse would have been dark and smoky.

Many roundhouses had a section set aside for animals. Sheep, goats and even small cattle would be kept inside, especially in the winter months, as shown archaeologically by finds of animal dung and hoof prints and other marks. Providing heat and milk, the animals would have contributed to the rich mixture of smells inside the roundhouse. The only toilets for the resident humans would have been pots, emptied daily into a nearby midden, which would have made the inside of the roundhouse even smellier. Archaeological discoveries in these middens have revealed much about Iron Age diets.

Closer to the fire – the best place for light and warmth – would have been the activity areas. In the summer months, and in the limited winter daylight, most activities would take place outside. Clearly differentiated working spaces are regularly discovered by archaeologists, for example circles of manufacturing debris where groups worked on different crafts over many years. Some larger roundhouses appear to have had upstairs areas, wooden platforms for sleeping, which would have benefited from the rising heat of the fire for warmth and pest reduction, as well as keeping the ground floor space clearer for other activities.

The farming year and the religious festivals that marked it governed people's lives. The majority of Iron Age communities were subsistence farmers, looking after a small area of mixed farmland supporting animals and crops. Most farmers grew wheat and barley and kept cattle, sheep and pigs. Some farming families spent part of their time making salt, quern stones or iron. These essentials were traded across Britain over long distances, while other essentials were grown or made locally. Most settlements have archaeological evidence of making clothes, woodworking and even blacksmithing. Luxuries, such as shale bracelets, pots, bronze objects, animal furs and feathers were also traded over long distances.

Work

Discussion of home environments inevitably raises issues of contrasting 'work' spaces. The industrialised world model is that of distinctive 'home' and 'work' environments, defined partly by being physically separate and thus requiring travel to and fro, even if only over a very short distance, but primarily by being physically distinctive, with a totally different use of space, social differentiation and hierarchy. This is a very modern, industrialised and increasingly challenged model. It is, in fact, an exceptionally specific cultural model rather than a norm, whose definitions arose in a few places after the Industrial Revolution that began in Britain in the later eighteenth century. Both in the past and the present, the norm is for much less differentiated spaces equally suited to living, working and relaxing. The distinctions come, rather, from different *types* of living and working in an organic, flexible space. Differentiations can be drawn, for example, between cottage industry living/working spaces, farming living/working spaces, or even more subtly blended living/working spaces, such as farmers whose families also produce additional materials for home consumption and sale or barter. The industrialised, differentiated model of living/working is increasingly under threat. With the rise of portable computer technology and an ever-more service-driven business model, work in such societies is less dependent on large numbers of employees being based in one place to physically produce objects and increasingly dependent on people working partly or fully at home or in other communal spaces, for example, social spaces such as coffee shops.

For the vast majority of the present human population, now as in the past, discussions of home–work balance are irrelevant: home and work are one and the same and revolve around variations of subsistence living, mixed farming and industrial activity, with few efficiencies of scale, undertaken in or close to the home. The only major difference between communities in the past and the present lies not in their immediate home/work/ living environment but rather in the impact of the industrialised world on their lives. Subsistence farming communities not only grow crops for their own consumption or relatively local sale or barter, but also specific crops sold for cash, providing materials that are destined to end up in the industrialised world. But this should not lead us to assume that there was no *differentiation* of space in these intermixed home–work environments in the past.

One of the world's earliest industrialised landscapes is the Ironbridge Gorge in Shropshire, England, near the modern city of Birmingham. This small riverside town was home to successive generations of the Darby family (including Abraham Darby, 1678–1717) which was instrumental in perfecting the technique of smelting iron ore with coke in a blast furnace. This meant iron production was much cheaper, which led to more sophisticated iron designs and uses and the ushering in of the Industrial Revolution that continues to influence every aspect of the world to this day. The site of Ironbridge is globally recognised as the home of the Industrial Revolution and in 1986 it was named as a UNESCO World Heritage Site to mark this status. Ironbridge has a wealth of surviving buildings (including houses and former ironworking and other industrial sites) and infrastructure, most notably its distinctive iron bridge built between 1777 and 1781 to link the communities on both banks of the River Severn. Within a few miles of one another along the valley are a series of different and exceptionally well-preserved industrial landscapes connected to Ironbridge's early history and subsequent development. Some of these sites are still being explored archaeologically.

This is one of the best surviving and earliest industrial landscapes in the world, precursor to the often much larger industrial landscapes that litter the earth today. Archaeological work in the area since the 1970s has revealed tremendous amounts about its early industrial origins, as well as about the communities that undertook such work. Metallurgical analyses of manufacturing

Figure 7 The Iron Bridge and village of Ironbridge in Shropshire, the birthplace of the global Industrial Revolution (copyright and courtesy of Paul Belford)

residues from different sites are particularly important, offering an insight into ancient manufacturing processes that can be compared with those at other locations near and far. The scientific techniques developed to help analyses of such materials have a wider applicability on other archaeological sites with metal residues of other periods and cultures.

Ritual and religion

If there is confusion in differentiating 'home' from 'work' spaces in the archaeological record, a consideration of other aspects of the material evidence of our lives is even more frustrating. Nowhere is this truer than in the consideration of the evidence of ritual or religious spaces and materials.

For many people in the modern world, the issue of religion may seem outwardly clear, at least at first. The plethora of distinctive 'religious' locations that are outside people's immediate home and work environments and which require travel to get to, even if only a walk along a road, seem to mark them out as special. Inside, such spaces are clearly very different from either homes or workplaces. However, a deeper consideration of these locations raises a host of complications, to do with:

- *Spatial and social differentiation within ritual facilities* – some people work in ritual spaces: clergy and more prosaic workers, such as cleaning and maintenance staff. Religious spaces are thus working places for some. Other people come to worship there; the worship thus blends work and leisure, dependent on the context of religious observation. Many such spaces also have defined areas that can be accessed or to which entry is barred, based on things such as social status, sex, age or simply personal preference.
- *Portable ritual evidence* – people carry many different symbolic ritual materials, such as different types of amulet, brooch, necklace or copies of religious texts that can be used in varied forms in almost any environment. In daily life, as well as at extremes, almost anywhere can become a ritual or religious site, often only very briefly and for the individual rather than the group.
- *Home ritual evidence* – many people have religious materials of some sort in their home or workplace, from simple religious materials, to texts fixed on walls, to dedicated places for ritual or religious activity. Linked to the issue of bathing and cleaning spaces, many modern and ancient religions include ritualised bathing elements associated with the cycle of prayer and religious observation. In some cases bathing is highly complicated, involving clearly defined and organised ritual bathing facilities. Under such circumstances, a bath is not necessarily just a simple form of cleaning or leisure.

- *Intangible ritual materials* – the ultimate complication is that, by their very nature, some aspects of ritual and religion leave no evidence. Although countless religious buildings and other structures exist, almost all religions include an element of personal reflection, prayer or contemplation, which leaves little or no physical trace. This can be particularly true in the ritual aspects of behaviour that influence our daily lives, from specific diets to prayer and meditation. This leads to the archaeology of *contemplation*, of looking for the subtle evidence of such daily ritual through the presence of materials such as prayer mats and stools, religious works, portable shrines and altars, and devotional objects.

THE CHANGING FACE OF HAGIA SOPHIA

Christian churches and Islamic mosques have served a variety of purposes for their communities for millennia. They include a variety of formal and informal spaces designed both for different rituals and for more general social uses. Within the environs of churches and mosques lie spaces that can be highly differentiated, depending on the status, age or gender of individuals, the type of ritual or social activity taking place, the time of year or even the time of day.

The ultimate example of similarities in spatial use between religions is the ancient ritual site of Hagia Sophia in Istanbul. Built as a Christian church in the sixth century CE (replacing an earlier series of structures begun in the fourth century CE), it became an Islamic mosque in 1453 CE before being turned into a museum in 1935 on the orders of Mustafa Kemal Atatürk, the first President and founder of the Republic of Turkey. The site's complex history has been painstakingly pieced together by archaeologists and archaeological fieldwork continues to reveal surprises about Hagia Sophia. One of the most spectacular finds of recent years was a series of ancient underground tunnels, alleged to connect the cathedral with the Basilica Cistern, Princes' Islands and Topkapi Palace. Fieldwork in the late 1990s found sealed passages, a graveyard full of children's bones and the burial chamber of Hagia Sophia's first priest, but the project also helped to prove that the passages did not lead to the Basilica Cistern and Princes' Islands.

Ritual and religion take many forms and the possibilities of misinterpretation of the physical evidence are legion. Sport serves as a modern example, being an undoubted form of ritual that also has many characteristics of a religion. These characteristics include clearly differentiated, and internally hierarchical, places for observation (stadiums), symbolic materials from written rules and texts to clothing and other identifiable or symbolic objects that can be used by individuals or carried, opportunities for observation in the home or elsewhere as part of daily life, cycles based around the calendar year, for example periods of inactivity or different activity or regular days for events throughout the year, and intangible aspects such as thinking and caring about the outcome of sporting events. This modern example has strong analogies with the social uses and material culture of sport in many ancient societies, for example ancient Greece and Rome, where sporting events served many different functions beyond simply being sports and leisure events, as forms of political display and as meeting places for business and leisure.

An informative take on some of these issues comes from the work of the American archaeologist Eleanor Harrison-Buck. In 2012 she published the results of her work exploring the distribution of marine shells used as architectural elements in ancient Mayan circular shrine architecture in Mesoamerica (roughly modern-day Mexico, Belize, Guatemala, El Salvador, Honduras, Nicaragua and Costa Rica). She suggested that, more than just symbols of sacredness, these materials represented living entities for their communities, animating the shrines through their ongoing relationships with human and other-than-human agents in the world, an analytical concept known as *animism* that stems from anthropological analyses of Indigenous communities. Such a perspective on the animation of ritual and religious sites has strong parallels with many other religions, for example the use of candles and incense in churches of the Catholic and Anglican Christian tradition, which similarly animate the religious activity in such churches; that is, they help to mediate the relationship between past and present communities as well as human and other than-human agents through their use. Such analyses help further archaeological analyses of religious sites when ostensibly mundane materials such as shells, candles or incense are discovered at them, materials that clearly had a much more important religious function beyond any strictly utilitarian explanation.

Leisure and relaxation

For the majority of human history it is clear that formally differentiated leisure time, space or activity was not the norm. For anything close to leisure to emerge required the emergence of elite groups that could take advantage of the work of others to free up their own time. It then took the expansion of industrialised mass production and technology to give similar leisure to a wider section of society. But today, many people around the world still have no formal leisure, in the accepted sense of regular time off or holidays away from their daily lives. None the less, this is an issue worth considering in terms of archaeology.

It is clear that, even without formal time allocation or facilities, humans can still relax and be 'at leisure' in various ways: simply sitting in the sun at the end of a working day, playing a makeshift game or engaging in a physical activity such as swimming. Such activities are important to humans both personally, in that having some time away from work when we are not doing household chores, eating or sleeping is important for mental and physical wellbeing, and communally, in that group activities like sport are important for social cohesion and training for work. Many sports have military origins and were originally about training in specific martial skills and improving physical fitness.

Extensive archaeological evidence exists for leisure activities at a small scale, including the remains of different types of games and toys. On the larger scale are facilities broadly attuned to leisure activities, places so extensive that they become all-encompassing working, living and leisure environments. The ultimate modern example is the US city of Las Vegas, which began life in the 1930s as a scatter of casinos, hotels, restaurants and related leisure facilities but which grew rapidly in the later twentieth century into a major city, albeit one still focused on providing leisure services. Other examples include the coastal resort towns of nineteenth and twentieth century Europe and the USA, originally built to serve the annual holidaymakers of nearby industrial communities. Such towns have an entire infrastructure built around leisure activities: promenades, piers and amusement parks. Their legacy lives on in modern-day locations such as the numerous Disney resorts around the world.

At a smaller scale are countless other leisure facilities that survive as individual buildings, either archaeologically or historically. The historical ones are present in many communities and offer intriguing possibilities of interpretation or – more commonly – misinterpretation. For example, many British towns and cities have former cinemas scattered about. In the 1950s these cinemas served local communities in terms of both leisure and work. Cinemas were inexpensive leisure facilities that showed films and cartoons but they simultaneously served a work function, in that they also played newsreels and so kept people informed of important events. With the advent of cheap radios and televisions, the need for such cinemas declined and many were demolished or adapted to other uses, as supermarkets, music venues and churches.

The boundaries of leisure and work blur under such circumstances. Such ambiguity of interpretation arises in other ostensibly leisure facilities. Pubs and bars, for example, abound around the world and serve a mixed leisure and work role, at once places to drink (often alcohol), socialise and relax and yet also places for the exchange of news and information and the forging of bonds, thus advancing both work and home agendas.

Two comparative examples of surviving historic leisure landscapes provide an insight both into the types of archaeological evidence that can survive and, crucially, indicate how such evidence can be approached with an archaeological mind. Both case studies show how one person with a particular vision can profoundly influence following generations, through their legacy affecting the modern, as much as the ancient, world. Both are also modern-day leisure spaces, generating millions of pounds of revenue annually from their visitors, a longevity of leisure use that their patrons, designers and builders never anticipated.

The great wealth accumulated by a small number of people as a result of the early industrialisation of Britain produced some of the finest examples of leisure landscapes. While a growing number were consigned to a depressing life working in the new industrial facilities, including mines (for raw materials like coal), ironworks (for machinery) and mills (for textile production), a small upper echelon of society spent the wealth created by these new industrial activities on impressively designed parks and gardens. These parks were part of large estates that usually included a grand country house and farms to provide food and generate additional income. Major sections of such estates were, in the hands of master designers like Lancelot 'Capability' Brown (1716–1783), turned from medieval hunting parklands (and often former medieval monastic estates) into elaborately designed landscape gardens including formal and informal areas, water features, ruins both real and ancient and modern facsimiles, and countless other features. Well-known surviving examples include Brown's parks at Blenheim in Oxfordshire, Stowe in Buckinghamshire and, most dramatic of all, Chatsworth in Derbyshire. These formal landscapes cost huge sums to design, build and maintain and are truly leisure landscapes, lacking any function. They were not designed to be productive in any real understanding of the term, and cost huge sums of money to build and maintain to no economic benefit; not even generating income from visitors, as many do now.

Landscape-scale archaeological analyses of these locations have led to a new understanding of the complexity of such sites' development, both of the scale of the planning and reordering of the existing landscape and also of the phases of change, with multiple leisure landscapes overlapping and intermingling as styles and tastes changed. Archaeology also reveals distinct areas of activity, including support infrastructure (for example, pipes to move water around a site) and technological innovation (for example, the emergence and development of greenhouses). There is also evidence for some radical experimentation, such as the development of 'pineapple houses', special facilities for the cultivation of this exotic fruit, which, originating in South America, had to be carefully cultivated in specially heated facilities to survive in Britain's much colder climate. The remains of such facilities have been identified by archaeologists at several sites, such as within the eighteenth-century walled garden at Amisfield in East Lothian, southern Scotland, as well as rare examples surviving as historic buildings, for example the extraordinary walled garden and structure known as the Pineapple near Airth in Falkirk, southern Scotland.

In contrast to the elite leisure landscapes of Capability Brown, a less well-known man was equally influential in the creation of some of the most popular and well-known leisure landscapes of the twentieth century: football grounds. What Capability Brown was to eighteenth-century parkland landscapes, Archibald Leitch (1865–1939) was to twentieth-century football stadiums. Leitch designed many of Britain's most iconic football stadiums and consequently influenced the underlying form and format of stadiums for all sorts of sports around the world to the present day. Leitch's work survives on more than twenty sites in Britain, including the old Arsenal stadium in north London, Fulham in west London, the old Dell stadium in Southampton, Hampden Park and Ibrox in Glasgow, Hillsborough in Sheffield and Old Trafford in Manchester, to name just six of his most famous examples.

Leitch was effectively responsible for the spread and popularisation of many classic components of the modern-day football stadium, including turnstile entrances, wooden fold-down terraced seating in two-tier covered stands and many other innovations that survive in some form to this day. However, other Leitch innovations never caught on, especially his stand-alone 'club houses' containing changing rooms and a separate viewing stand for club officials. One of the few remaining examples survives almost untouched at Fulham Football Club's Craven Cottage stadium in west London, which is now a listed building, recognised as being of national importance and protected accordingly by law. In his own way, Leitch was as, if not more, influential in the creation of leisure landscapes than people like Capability Brown. The impact of people like Leitch on the modern world is increasingly being recognised and studied with an archaeological mindset.

Social order, governance, law and the military

Across human history, social dynamics have led to hierarchies, organisations and other evidence of social control. In prehistory, such places are often very hard to detect and can only be identified through careful long-term analysis of the landscape.

At Stonehenge, in central southern England, analyses over the last decade (most recently different forms of remote sensing) have continued to reveal new evidence about the role of Stonehenge as a ritual – including social governance – centre in prehistory.

The main monument sits within a complex landscape of features that stretched as far as the Avebury stone circle some 24 miles to the north, and in which the movement of people along ritual routes between the different structures and locations was central to social control in different periods.

Even for more recent periods the archaeological evidence for social governance can be fragmentary. A project undertaken by the Universities of Winchester and Nottingham and University College, London, led by the medieval archaeologist Andrew Reynolds, showed Anglo-Saxon communities of the fifth to eleventh centuries CE clearly placed great importance on outdoor meeting places for broadly political activities but precisely what went on there, and even what physical or topographic characteristics, if any, defined them, remains unclear, since only a dozen or so such sites have been investigated by archaeologists.

Studying such meeting places and their surroundings reveals much about their relationship to other social functions and places. The project led by Reynolds brought together archaeology, place-name analysis and written sources in the first national study of such sites, which were crucial to arbitration, negotiation and dispute settlement between the emerging kingdoms of England. Place names of assembly sites and their associated districts indicate, for example, varying origins, in some cases referring to pre-Christian gods including Woden and Thor, in others relating to monuments of earlier ages, such as burial mounds and standing stones. For other periods there are clearer traces; for example, there are facilities for law-making and, broadly, politics and political debate, such as debating chambers and meeting rooms. In association with these, facilities existed where civil servants and other support staff could work and live.

Another historic side of governance was the housing of members of the ruling elite in castles and palaces, where social activities played an important part in daily life. Consequently, facilities for large social gatherings and display abound in such places, most notably around the Mediterranean in ancient Egypt, Greece and Rome, where large ceremonial sites such as forums, agorae and similar survive in large numbers. In contrast, the military can overlap with governance and law and yet remain distinctive. Thousands of castles dating from the Middle Ages are scattered across Europe, ranging from the austere to the luxurious in terms of internal layout and facilities, depending on the intentions and whims of their owners. Alternatively, there are specific sites for military testing, both for offensive and defensive actions. These include everything from coastal watchtowers to atomic weapon test sites by way of thousands of other possible military uses, including the prosaic infrastructure of the military, the facilities and supply chains needed to feed, clothe, clean, transport and arm the military, irrespective of their activities.

Perhaps the best-studied ancient equivalent of this infrastructure is Hadrian's Wall in northern Britain, where a wide range of facilities survives in the archaeological record that has been intensively analysed since the 1950s. Begun in 122 CE, during the rule of Emperor Hadrian, and largely complete within six years, the wall eventually extended to 80 Roman miles (73 statute miles or 120 km) long. Archaeological excavations have shown that the Wall was part of a wider defensive system which, from north to south, included: a row of forts five to ten miles north of the Wall, used for scouting and intelligence; a *glacis* (artificial slope) and deep associated ditch; a *berm* (raised barrier separating two areas) with rows of pits holding entanglements; the curtain wall itself (the best-surviving of all of these elements); a military road; and, finally, the *vallum*, a long earthwork and ditch that ran the entire length of the wall as an additional defence.

A number of the forts along the Wall have been subject to intensive archaeological investigation, including Housesteads, Banna (Birdoswald), Vindolanda and Segedunum (Wallsend).

Figure 8 Mile castle 39 (also known as Castle Nick), a Roman fortification along Hadrian's Wall, occupied until the late fourth century CE (copyright and courtesy of Sarah Dhanjal)

They have revealed a lot about daily life on the Wall, in particular formal and informal modifications to its infrastructure. For example, due to the lie of the land, Housesteads' orientation is unorthodox, in that its long axis is arranged parallel with Hadrian's Wall, which forms its northern defence. It is also unusual in that it had no running water and depended on collecting rainwater, for which purpose a series of large stone-lined tanks lined the periphery of the defences. In contrast, Banna (Birdoswald) shows an unbroken sequence of occupation on the site of the fort granaries; two successive large timber halls replaced the granaries as late as 500 CE. It has been suggested that, after the end of Roman rule in Britain, the fort served as the power base for a local war band descended from the late Roman garrison. At Vindolanda, a *vicus* (a self-governing village) developed to the west of the fort. The vicus contained several rows of buildings, each containing several one-room chambers. To the south of this fort lay a large Roman bathhouse complex.

A different example of how the impact of social order on the past can be identified through archaeology comes from a consideration of the varied uses of medieval and post-medieval castles. The traditional view of such sites is that they were built primarily for military reasons, as both defensive and offensive structures. However, some archaeologists argue that the primary motive behind such construction and modification was, rather, the expression of social status and that this social status is reflected in their location, design and interior layout. Kenilworth Castle in Warwickshire, England, is an excellent example of the mixed purposes to which a castle could be put. The archaeologist Matthew Johnson exhaustively examines this castle in his 2013 book, *Behind the Castle Gate*, demonstrating the gradual but extensive modification of the original twelfth-century defensive fortress through the thirteenth, fourteenth and fifteenth centuries, in which the castle changed from a primarily military structure into a primarily palatial one. By the 1570s the castle had become a fully fledged Renaissance palace, albeit one capable, if need be, of serious defence in the event of a siege. The castle had grown, over the course of several hundred years, from a fairly modest beginning (most probably as a simple motte and bailey design) to the extensive structure that exists to this day as ruins, sitting within a much wider landscape. The modification of this landscape, especially its evolution from a primarily defensive to a primarily leisure environment, is as important to the understanding of the site as the castle itself. And those modifications can only be understood through intensive archaeological analyses, especially different forms of landscape survey.

Figure 9 Kenilworth Castle, Warwickshire. The photograph was taken in January 2008 after heavy rain, when the fields were slightly flooded. Until around 1650 there would have been a much deeper sheet of water here (copyright and courtesy of Brian Kerr)

5
The archaeology
of landscapes

The next time you fly somewhere, make sure that you get a window seat and take the opportunity to look down on the land beneath you. As your aeroplane rises to its cruising altitude, a giant jigsaw puzzle of landscape emerges, from the facilities and infrastructure of the airport that you have just left and expanding to surrounding towns and cities, farmland and coastlines. Further afield, in places such as the sections of north-eastern Canada that most transatlantic flights cross, lie apparently endless tracts of sub-arctic tundra, snow and ice-fields into which it looks as if humans have never ventured. Flying above such landscapes, the relationship of one community to another, or the transition from one environment to another, seem easy enough to perceive. But imagine how difficult this analysis would be without the benefits of being up in an aeroplane; an experience that people dreamed of for generations before the emergence of powered flight in the early twentieth century.

A major research focus of archaeology is the understanding of entire landscapes; landscapes that are dozens, hundreds or even thousands of miles in extent. Dealing with archaeology at this scale means grappling with the issues confronted at the small scale but also coming to terms with some distinctive new issues associated with how humans have interacted with, and transformed, landscapes over the millennia. Landscapes are palimpsests, showing the cumulative effects of processes at different scales and tempos over time. Most elements of a landscape are historical and stratified, just like smaller, single archaeological sites. A key question is always: would an ancient occupant of a landscape under analysis have recognised it as a defined and distinctive 'place' or 'space'?

Landscape-scale archaeological methodologies also have to consider the realities of surveying large sites. The methodologies are used to help decide whether to use different forms of remote sensing or more laborious but potentially more revealing methods, such as various field-walking techniques. This leads on to further questions of the merits of relative sampling strategies; that is, how much of and where in a landscape to sample. In a different context, landscape methodologies question what evidence has been irretrievably lost, or sites destroyed, by both natural (for example, coastal erosion, desertification or flooding) and cultural (for example, urban expansion) processes. It is questions such as these that archaeologists attempt to answer in landscape analyses, through the intensive investigation of whole landscapes to identify patterns of resource control, distribution and re-distribution.

Scale and definition in the landscape

Prosaically, the issue of scale means trying to understand the rough extent of the ancient landscape – or at least, a portion of it – under analysis, if only because this is important in setting the methodological boundaries of an investigation. This affects, in turn, the types of tools deployed by the archaeologists. Analyses of scale also mean understanding the different levels of definition of past land-use impact that can be seen, especially distinguishing between intensive and extensive land use, by comparing the different remnants left by humans on their landscape.

It is important to avoid cultural stereotyping. The industrialised world is heavily urbanised, and so biased towards urbanism. We tend to perceive urbanism as implying cultural sophistication; cultures such as the Indigenous cultures of many countries, with no communities that are identifiably urban in the Western sense, have in the past been seen as less sophisticated. This is a fatal misunderstanding of those communities, which have had every bit as big an impact on their environment as Western towns and cities. However, these impacts are, to Western, urban eyes, subtler in terms of their immediate physical impact.

The archaeology of settlement hierarchies is another key issue as regards the scale of the archaeology of landscape. When considering social relations, structuration and place, it is interesting to note that the differentiations between larger places – entire settlements – are made on the basis of the same key social markers of age, sex, social class and income we have discussed elsewhere.

Picking up such differentiations at the small scale, in individual homes or neighbourhoods, is one thing but what about at the scale of an entire landscape? Most people can identify variations in relative wealth and social status between different properties in their immediate neighbourhood, on the basis of evidence such as the relative size of a house or the value of the cars parked outside it. But what about differentiating between the relative wealth of different cities? This is a much harder proposition. Such differentiations are often visible in the past in the archaeological record; comparing, for example, the relative sizes and spatial distribution of properties within an ancient village. Analyses of the remains of materials found within properties in different locations further distinguishes such landscape-scale differentiation. As an example, archaeologists might, through the analysis of discarded bones, identify evidence of variations in diet between different communities not just in the types of foods being consumed but also the different cuts of meat being eaten. Such differences in diet and preference are key markers of relative social status among different groups.

Complexity and cognition in the landscape

Understanding complexity in the landscape means appreciating the overlapping physical and mental landscapes over time and among different peoples. It is rare for there to be simply one landscape and for that landscape to be clearly physically defined. Rather, different communities experience the same landscape simultaneously in different ways, both physical and mental. Archaeology has to grapple with peoples' perceptions of their environment as reflected through their physical remains.

Consider the Indigenous peoples of Australia. Their communities' cultural perception and identity, in terms of both physical and mental environments, is deeply connected to what is commonly referred to as the 'Dreamtime' or the 'Dreaming'. The Dreaming sums up the communities' understanding of the creation of their people and their landscape. It is central to their cultural world view and self-perception and intimately connected to the physical landscape. The Dreaming provides a manner of perceiving the interlinked physical and mental landscapes of the past and present, in ways so alien to Western perception that they are hard for us to fully grasp. Such perceptions require us to abandon all Western senses of chronological time, linearity and space. These perceptions must be replaced by a far more holistic sense of people and place, set in a complicated plane of living, in which the past and present blend, and within which our ancestors are active participants in a combined mental and physical landscape. In this landscape, not only time and space but also the natural and cultural environments blend. This attitude explains the relatively light physical footprint (in Western terms) these communities leave on the landscape. The presence of people was in fact profound, but they left a very different type of trace than Western expectations might have predicted.

The failure of Western communities to appreciate the deep interconnectedness of the Indigenous people of Australia and their landscape (both mental and physical) has caused many problems between Indigenous and European Australian cultures, in the past as well as the present. For example, to this day, land ownership claims on the basis of ancestral use are much harder for Indigenous communities to make. The legal system is biased in favour of physical evidence of land use but Indigenous communities often used specific places for activities that left no, or only very subtle, physical traces, or activities which only specific social or gender groups can know about, discuss or share in public. This is referred to as 'intangible cultural heritage' and is an increasingly important part of modern-day heritage management involving archaeologists, as reflected in the 2003 UNESCO Convention for the Safeguarding of Intangible Cultural Heritage.

Data and evidence types in the landscape

More and more work in landscape research is done not by physically collecting data in the environment but rather by working in the laboratory. Environmental archaeologists spend much time analysing the minute remains of ancient plant pollen recovered from sites, while climatologists analyse changes that happened over millennia by studying ice cores. Many different specialists routinely use sophisticated computer models to plot changes in data and model human behaviours in different environments or in response to different environmental scenarios. The sheer quantity and interconnectedness of landscape data helps provide a better understanding of the significance and relationship between the different elements that make up the environment, both cultural (for example, human, including past and present activities) and natural (for example, environmental, such as flora and fauna).

Landscape archaeologists have increasingly turned to ever more sophisticated remote-sensing tools. The traditions of intensive landscape surveys conducted by teams of people based in a landscape for weeks or months have been joined by satellite survey data, particularly LIDAR. LIDAR picks up every hump and bump to create high-resolution digital elevation models of archaeological sites, which can reveal topography otherwise hidden by vegetation. One particularly useful advance is the use of Geographic Information Systems (GIS) – software that stores, edits and displays geographic information. GIS can be used to plot multiple different and overlapping layers of environmental data on past and present landscapes. Such models allow archaeologists to visualise changing sea levels and thus coastlines, as well as shifts in farming patterns through crop changes, as indicated from pollen samples, which can in turn indicate long-term changes in climate and change in land use over time. This process, known as 'Historic Landscape Characterisation', applies a standardised methodology to map historic landscape features in detail on a GIS. All these different issues can be considered either separately or in conjunction, using computer models for specific times or periods, or to consider change over the short, medium or long term. GIS layers can also be joined by particular types of additional data, both non-archaeological, such as the geology, and archaeological data, such as known find-spots and settlement sites.

Such data are useful both in researching archaeology and in managing and, importantly, preserving it. Knowing where archaeological sites exist, as well as using models to predict the locations of future sites, supports modern land-management activities, such as planning new settlements. These data also help plan responses to larger cycles of change in the environment, such as understanding which archaeological sites might be under threat from factors such as increased flood risk in seasonal storms, coastal erosion or desertification. Such data and analyses fit into a wider body of evidence used by governments to help large-scale landscape management, feeding global analyses of major environmental concerns and cultural issues such as food supply, population density and climate change.

Managing the landscape in the past and the present

Archaeologists in the twenty-first century work in close contact with researchers, government officers, planners and many other interested groups and individuals in the understanding and management of the environment. They help to ensure that all aspects of an environment, from archaeological remains to biological diversity, are maintained for future generations. Such management means undertaking interlinked planning. For instance, work might take place on archaeological sites only at certain times of year, so as not to disturb certain animal species at key breeding times or damage specific plants at a particular point in their growth. Planning can also mean making historic sites more suitable for specific plants and animals. Different plans for managed wetland, for example, can both protect an archaeological site and also encourage particular types of plant or animal to thrive alongside it; building different types of animal hides and roosts within historic buildings can protect both. Bat roosts, for example, are a common sight in many ruins but other roosts exist, such as habitats in historic barns for different species of owl. Such types of environmental protection and regulation can cut both ways, protecting historic sites while restricting access.

It is important to remember that many natural features are also human features. Some British hedgerows (thick hedges used as field borders in certain regions of the UK) are hundreds of years old, and relate to ancient property boundaries. In the 1950s, many of these hedges were destroyed to create the larger fields needed to operate larger farm machinery effectively. Such hedgerows are both cultural and natural; they are an important record of ancient farming practices and land ownership and a crucial element of the natural environment, preserving many different plant species and providing a habitat for animals, from tiny insects to large mammals. In recent years we have begun to appreciate how crucial hedgerows are to the overall balance of the environment, providing a habitat for natural pest controllers such as the insects and animals that live off common crop pests. Removing hedgerows literally harms the crops they surround.

Evidence for the environment and the landscape, therefore, comes at every possible scale and includes both archaeological data, such as artefacts manufactured by humans and, crucially, ecofacts: the seeds, plants and pollen remains that indicate particular activities, such as farming, that are large-scale modifiers of the environment. Using such data, it is possible to identify different types of large-scale landscape modification. One such landscape-level modification is the nuclear-test landscapes of the Pacific. These are among some of the most terrifying military landscapes in the world, made all the more sinister by their outward tranquillity. These sites are sometimes referred to as the 'Pacific Proving Grounds' in specific reference to the US atomic weapons test sites that were spread across the Marshall Islands of Micronesia. The first of these tests, Operation Crossroads, which took place on Bikini Atoll in 1946, included static, air-dropped and underwater detonations of atomic weapons to test their impact on various different types of landscape and military equipment. The submerged wrecks of the Operation Crossroads site were subject to a detailed archaeological assessment by the US National Parks Service in the early 1990s. These surveys tested for radioactive contamination and also surveyed the impact of the tests on the wrecks, many of which had not, for obvious reasons, previously been explored by divers. This work revealed, among other things, how difficult it is to destroy a vessel using atomic weapons; ships within the immediate blast radius were destroyed, and many sank as a result of damage and the tidal wave created by the explosion, but few vessels were entirely destroyed by the concussive effects of the explosion in the water.

The French government also tested atomic weapons at two main sites in the Pacific, in the Tuamotu Archipelago, between 1966 and 1996, as did Britain in the early 1950s at a variety of sites in what is now the Republic of Kiribati. Many of these test sites remain dangerous to this day, due to the high levels of residual radioactivity. Due to this radioactivity, as well as the continuing veil of government secrecy, most of these sites have not been subject to archaeological investigation. But the legacy of the tests can be felt around the world, in the dispossessed communities of these islands, which were forcibly moved *en masse* to other locations to clear the ground for the tests, and in the prevalence of cancer and other illnesses among the service personnel who were present. The traces of these tests will be with us for many generations and will reach far beyond the Pacific landscapes that they transformed.

Perceptions of the environment

Within different environments, a fascinating body of evidence exists for differing perceptions of the environment in the past, through things such as the physical remains of art, documentary records (for example, records of crops or lunar cycles) and intangible heritage such as songs and stories. Some ancient communities clearly spent a tremendous amount of time simply observing and thinking about the environment in the broadest sense, and left some of the most perplexing physical remains, both individual locations and complicated, managed ritual environments.

Figure 10 The ship is the most common figurative motif in Scandinavian rock art (copyright and courtesy of Courtney Nimura)

Around the coastlines of modern–day Scandinavia lie thousands of fragments of prehistoric rock art, usually engravings into naturally exposed rock faces, sometimes enhanced and highlighted with pigments. Such art depicts the wide array of flora and fauna that surrounded the communities, the people themselves and their tools. Figure 10 shows one example of this type of art, from Hornes Mellom in Østfold, south–east Norway. In the Bronze Age, twenty-two ships and an additional fifteen small pits (called cup marks) were carved on this natural rock outcrop. Vertical lines indicate crew members and the ships are depicted with double stems with ornamental prows, reminiscent of the Danish Hjortspring boat from the Pre-Roman Iron Age, dating from about 400–300 BCE. The eleven ships and two cup marks pictured in Figure 10 were painted by the Norwegian heritage agency to make the carvings more visible.

In his 1997 book, *Rock Art and the Prehistory of Atlantic Europe*, the archaeologist Richard Bradley showed that, above all, this art is exceptionally open: both curious about the environment but also very much part of the environment. The favoured rock faces are usually at natural viewpoints and many are in coastal locations. They often have springs that run water across some or all of the area. This is not art that is hidden away; it is very much outward-looking and part of the environment. Bradley argues that these carvings should be interpreted as a series of symbolic messages shared among monuments, artefacts and natural places in the landscape. The art has a cultural setting in the landscape and can be interpreted in relation to ancient land use, the creation of ritual monuments and the burial of the dead. Such art thus played a vital role in shaping the way in which our ancestors viewed the natural world and the landscape they inhabited.

It is worth noting that almost all ancient communities were fascinated by cosmology and its impact on the environment, especially the cycles of the moon and the yearly change in the seasons. From the cosmological paintings of the Indigenous peoples of Australia, to the manuscript lists observing such changes made by medieval European monks, by way of the dramatic physical landscape remains of sites such as Stonehenge in England and the Nazca lines of Peru, there are many examples of interest in the landscape and of external impacts on the landscape. What this discussion comes down to is this: *people* make places and, as a consequence, there are no natural places left on earth, not anywhere, not even in the deepest oceans or the most remote or exposed corners of the world. The question that archaeologists ask is that of scale: how *significant* has our physical impact been on different places over time and can these effects – and their changes – be identified in the landscape?

If there are no 'natural' places left then many different *types* of landscape still exist and are studied by archaeologists. Some examples are discussed in greater detail below but the questions that archaeologists ask about these include issues such as:

ENVIRONMENTAL CHANGE AND THE VIKING SETTLEMENT OF NORTH AMERICA

An intriguing archaeological study of the impact of environmental change on settlement patterns comes from L'Anse aux Meadows, an archaeological site on the northernmost tip of Newfoundland in Canada. Discovered in 1960, it is the only known site of a Viking Age village in Canada and, indeed, the whole of North America. Dating from around 1000 CE, L'Anse aux Meadows is notable for its possible connection with the attempted colonisation of Vinland by Leif Ericson at around the same time, and more broadly with Norse exploration of the Americas.

Archaeological excavation at the site was conducted in the 1960s under the direction of Parks Canada, the Canadian national park service. This work uncovered the remains of eight buildings constructed of earth and grass sods placed over wooden frames. Based on associated artefacts, the buildings have variously been identified as dwellings or workshops. The largest dwelling measured 30 x 15 m (95 x 51 ft) and consisted of several rooms. Workshops were also identified, including an iron smithy containing a forge and iron slag, a carpentry workshop and a specialised boat repair area containing worn rivets.

The archaeological evidence suggests that the Norse inhabited the site for only a relatively short time. Primarily, the site was simply too isolated. The nearest settlements were further north, in Greenland, in a series of three interlinked colonies of roughly the same period as L'Anse aux Meadows. Ruins of more than six hundred farms have been found in these settlements – five hundred in the Eastern settlement, ninety-five in the Western settlement and twenty in the Middle – putting the tiny scale of the single settlement at L'Anse aux Meadows in perspective. Despite their much larger scale, the Greenland colonies also failed, around 1450 to 1500 CE, due to factors such as cumulative environmental damage, gradual climate change, conflicts with hostile Indigenous neighbours, the loss of contact and support from Europe, and cultural conservatism and the consequent failure to adapt to an increasingly harsh natural environment.

For a considerable time the relatively warm West Greenland current that flowed northwards along the south-western coast of Greenland made it feasible for the Norse to farm much as did their relatives in Iceland or northern Norway. But palynological (the study of spores, pollen and similar structures) tests of pollen counts and fossilised plants prove that the Greenlanders must have struggled with soil erosion and deforestation. Analyses of oxygen isotopes from the ice caps also suggest that the Medieval Warm Period (from about 950 to 1250 CE) caused a relatively milder climate in Greenland that lasted roughly from 800 to 1200. From 1300 or so the climate began to cool and by 1420 the Little Ice Age (a period of cooling that occurred after the Medieval Warm Period, between approximately 1350 and 1850) reached intense levels in Greenland. As the winters lengthened and the springs and summers shortened, this made life in the settlements harder and harder, forcing more and more reliance on hunting and gathering rather than farming; bone samples from Norse cemeteries in Greenland confirm that the proportion of sea animals in the typical Greenlander's diet increased from about twenty percent to eighty percent by the mid fourteenth century.

- *Short-, medium- and long-term change and human responses to such change*: short-term changes are usually the result of disasters such as volcanic eruptions and earthquakes, which usually leave significant physical traces and extremely visible impacts on physical structures. Medium-term and long-term changes are more complicated, for example, long-term natural environmental changes such as gradual shifts and/or cycles in climate, where traces may be found both of the changes themselves and also human responses to such change.

- *Extremes of environment and human responses to such extremes*: very cold or hot, wet or dry environments have impacts on human behaviour as well as the nature of surviving archaeological evidence. Extremely damp environments, such as seabeds, bogs and marshes preserve organic remains like wood and skin by sealing them in low-oxygen conditions that slow bacteriological decay. Likewise, extremely dry environments such as deserts or high and arid mountain regions desiccate materials, similarly providing an unfriendly environment for the bacteria and insects that would otherwise consume organic materials. Such extremes of environment also foster variations in human responses that can be studied, including different types of clothing and housing, different ways of preparing and preserving food and even different types of social, especially ritual, activity.

• *Human responses to environmental cycles*: another way of looking at the issue of different types of environment is to consider how humans respond to regular cycles. This includes the changing tides of each monthly lunar cycle, the changing light and life of the different seasons of the year and the gradual, almost imperceptible, cycles of climate that take place over centuries and millennia.

Sometimes the best way to appreciate a landscape is to come across one unexpectedly. The study of submerged prehistoric landscapes is a case in point; a largely unknown environment that is of profound significance for the understanding of prehistoric society. Research into such landscapes links landscape archaeology to advances in the latest technology, maritime to terrestrial archaeology and academia to big business.

The term 'submerged prehistoric landscape' refers to prehistoric environments that became submerged at the end of the last Ice Age, from approximately twenty thousand to eight thousand years ago (that is, between around 18,000 and 6000 BCE). Across the world, the great ice sheets that covered much of the world began to thaw, flooding the world with billions of litres of fresh water, raising sea levels by up to 120 metres and creating, by and large, the modern coastlines that we are familiar with.

For a variety of reasons, many people – including a startling number of archaeologists – are unaware of the extent or significance of such landscapes. But recently, fieldwork around the southern North Sea in north-west Europe has begun to redress this bias by highlighting the extent of information available from submerged prehistoric landscapes of the region. Such discoveries have major implications for other submerged zones around the world and have transformed our understanding of prehistoric societies' lifestyles, environments and technologies.

The history of the study of the submerged landscapes of the North Sea dates back to the nineteenth century, when recoveries of prehistoric materials such as stone tools and worked animal bone in the nets of fishermen came to the attention of antiquarians. In particular, finds from the area of shallow water in the middle of the North Sea, known as Dogger Bank, caught the attention of scholars, especially Clement Reid, who went on to publish the first book on this topic in 1913, entitled *Submerged Forests*. But it was only really in the 1970s that serious work on analysing such materials began and only in the 1990s that the full potential of this area's submerged prehistoric archaeology was realised. This transformation was in large part thanks to the work of the archaeologist Bryony Coles, who in 1998 coined the term 'Doggerland' for this lost prehistoric landscape. Since that time, with the benefit of new tools and enhanced industrial relations with marine industries, archaeologists have filled in the detail of this environment.

One project – the North Sea Palaeolandscapes Project – has, since the late 1990s, worked closely with the marine survey and aggregates industries to redraw in detail our understanding of this area, which at its largest extent was the size of the UK. The project analysed existing seismic survey data collected for the oil and gas industry by the company Petroleum Geo-Services (PGS). The result was a remarkable imaging of the entire palaeo-landscape of this zone, not just archaeological sites but a much more detailed and richer analysis of the geology and geomorphology, landscape, flora and fauna of the region, the subtleties of its landscape of flood plains and rivers, and its hilltops and slopes. These landscape analyses allowed further comparison with fine-grained archaeological data that could be used to indicate areas of high archaeological potential in the new landscape. The high-potential locations are those where discoveries of archaeological finds are more likely, given the conjunction of key environmental indicators of ancient settlement, such as those at sheltered former foreshore locations with a ready source of fresh water that would have made optimal prehistoric hunting sites. Such locations, once identified, can be subject to detailed investigation – including excavation – to examine their full potential.

Environmental change

Modelling environmental change involves the study of human responses to natural cycles of change and also of human impacts on (or modifications to) the environment over time. This area of research includes the intersection of archaeology with one of the hottest debates in contemporary society: climate change. Scientists, among them most archaeologists, point to detailed analyses of carbon dioxide (CO_2) levels dating back thousands of years that show a *gradual* increase in CO_2 over a long time but an *exponential* increase in such levels in the three hundred years since the Industrial Revolution, brought about the widespread burning of fossil fuels. Archaeologists place the evidence for CO_2 rises alongside similarly detailed environmental data for ancient climates around the world that reach back tens of thousands of years, collected from Arctic and Antarctic ice cores, and deeply buried environmental archaeological data such as the remains of insects and pollen. The correlation between a greater incidence of climate change and the growth of CO_2 emissions is marked, unmistakable and clearly human in origin. While there are undoubtedly broader patterns of short-, medium- and long-term naturally occurring climate change, the patterns of these natural cycles are modelled and understood and stand out in the overall record as quite different from human-generated climate change. The conclusion is simple: human activities that produce CO_2 are profoundly influencing the world's climate and at a greater and increasingly faster rate. There is no doubt about this general pattern. The only doubt among the scientific community (and the one that the climate change sceptics shamefully manipulate) is about the precise speed and intensity of this process and also how, or if, it can be controlled, reduced or mitigated.

In relation to these issues, in 2001, a new organisation, Scottish Coastal Archaeology and the Problem of Erosion (SCAPE), was set up to examine the threat of rising sea levels and the impact of coastal erosion on archaeological sites. Its aims are to research, conserve and promote the archaeology of Scotland's coast; as a consequence, SCAPE is especially interested in archaeological remains that are threatened by coastal erosion. Among other activities, SCAPE coordinates the Shorewatch Project, working with local groups to record and monitor sites that are under threat from environmental change. Scotland is particularly at risk from this problem; its fifteen-thousand-kilometre coastline is twice the length of the combined coastlines of England and Wales and is archaeologically rich. The low-lying sandy beaches that characterise much of the west coast are extremely fragile and vulnerable to loss in the storms that regularly occur in these exposed coastal locations, which are exposed to the full power of the North Atlantic.

Three examples drawn from the work of SCAPE demonstrate the types of sites at risk and the fieldwork that has been undertaken. At Sandwick, on the Isle of Unst in Shetland, an Iron Age settlement was discovered eroding from a small hillock on the beach. Already partially consumed by the sea, the remains of five structures were identified by a community archaeology group; the oldest structures date from the first millennium BCE and the most recent from the fifth century CE. At Cruester, on the Isle of Bressay, also in Shetland, a Bronze Age burnt mound was discovered eroding from the foreshore. In this case, the surviving stones of the mound were moved to a new, safer location adjacent to the local heritage centre, becoming part of a wider visitor attraction and an educational resource.

Baile Sear, an island in North Uist, part of the Outer Hebrides, was the site of two Iron Age 'wheelhouses'. In 2005, a severe storm struck the islands, removing up to 50 m of coastline overnight at some locations. The storm meant that these sites, formerly well inland, were now right on the foreshore, exposed by high tides and erosion of the beach dunes. The local community took the lead on the gradual excavation of the site in advance of its loss. Communities are central to the success of SCAPE's work; the length and remoteness of the coast means that the best way that sites can be excavated and monitored – especially after big storms – is by local communities.

The now-submerged lands between modern-day Russia and North America are an instructive but little-known example of how much landscapes populated by humans have changed over the long term. The existence of Beringia was verified both geologically and archaeologically from the 1960s onwards. This was a crucial landscape, across which the first settlers of the continent of America moved, until the Bering land bridge was inundated for the last time some time shortly after ten thousand years ago (about 8000 BCE). Increasing amounts of direct archaeological evidence for such settlement has been recovered in recent years, with the remains of extinct animals dredged up from the ocean floor and ancient river channels mapped within submerged sediments. Cores taken from the seabed of the area contain deposits such as peat that could only have been formed when it was dry land; these cores include insect remains that have been successfully dated.

This means that we now have a clear chronology for the development and eventual disappearance of the region, as well as an understanding of its environmental characteristics. As climate change makes the Arctic more and more accessible and the hunt for resources in this region expands, so more and more archaeological remains are likely to be discovered, refining our understanding of Beringia. Meanwhile, the broader contextual evidence of the archaeological potential of submerged prehistoric sites off the Pacific coast of the Americas – north, south and central – is huge. These remains are frequently located in areas where the marine geo-industry is undertaking surveys in the search for oil and gas reserves and where there is potential for collaborative explorations between archaeologists and industry of the type conducted in the North Sea.

These case studies are of long-term environmental change having a medium-term impact on specific archaeological sites. But to conclude this chapter, and as outlined earlier, there are also examples of short-term environmental change in the archaeological record. One of the least known but most dramatic examples of catastrophic environmental change is Port Royal, Jamaica, just across the bay from the modern city of Kingston. Now a tourist attraction and home to a small settlement, in the sixteenth and seventeenth centuries Port Royal was a major commercial centre for the Caribbean, a significant port city with more than six thousand inhabitants and two thousand buildings. Port Royal's contacts reached around the world, as did its notorious reputation as a haven for piracy and loose living. It has inspired many stories over the years, most recently the *Pirates of the Caribbean* film franchise.

The lively community life of Port Royal was brought to an abrupt end on 7 June 1692, when a devastating earthquake and tsunami hit the city, causing much of its northern section to collapse into the sea, killing hundreds of people and destroying many of the town's houses and other buildings, including the majority of its defences. The tsunami poisoned the land and the city's freshwater wells with salt water, rendering those parts of the town that survived the earthquake uninhabitable for years. Port Royal never recovered its former significance. Used as a naval base in the eighteenth and nineteenth centuries, in time it slipped into becoming the sleepy backwater it is today.

Another disastrous earthquake and tsunami on 14 January 1907 further damaged what was left of Port Royal. None the less, it remains a significant archaeological site, both above and below water, which has been studied since the 1950s. Underwater excavations in the 1980s and 1990s, led by Donny Hamilton of Texas A&M University, revealed the remarkably intact street pattern of the seventeenth-century town, including well-preserved houses complete with many household items. Some of these are mundane objects such as cooking pots and kitchen equipment but others are more exotic, including rare ceramics that would have been imported, at great expense, from China, which either indicates the exceptional wealth of some of the town's residents, or else is evidence of their pirate plunder. The archaeological investigations also revealed the fury of the original tsunami that destroyed the city; in one case, a small ship had been picked up and crashed into a house, both of which were submerged and then buried by the wave.

6

The archaeology
of travelling

A common misconception about the past is that people did not travel very much; that in this nasty, brutish and short life, the basic demands of daily living trapped people in one small area and that only a few (the elite, the intrepid and the foolhardy) ever ventured beyond the immediate horizon. This misconception is reinforced by Victorian mythologies about ancient peoples' misunderstanding of the world in terms of the shape, geography and extent of the earth, and thus the realistic possibilities of past travel. Archaeology reveals that people have been travelling for a very long time and, crucially, that they have left evidence of their travels.

The archaeology of travel is an increasingly important aspect of the analysis and investigation of the past. Some of the most ancient archaeological evidence in the world relates to this issue, particularly evidence for the global colonisation of the planet in deep prehistory, when biologically modern humans moved across the world from the cradle of humankind in central Africa. This movement was an extraordinary feat, especially in locations such as Australia and the South Pacific. Tens of thousands of years ago, movement in this region entailed repeated, open-water sea crossings (journeys that include part of the voyage being made out of sight of land), using vessels, since Australia and many of the Pacific islands were never connected to one another by land. This is completely different to locations such as Beringia, where land bridges allowed mass population movements. The evidence of the vessels themselves has not been discovered; the oldest remains of vessels found anywhere in the world so far date from a rather more modest 8000 BCE, at sites such as Uluburun off the southern coast of Turkey in the Mediterranean. But on the basis of dated materials from sites such as Lake Mungo in New South Wales, people were living in Australia at least forty thousand and possibly sixty thousand or more years ago. This means that people had to have travelled – and used vessels to travel – considerably before then. The archaeologist Robert Bednarik conducted several experiments in the late 1990s and early 2000s, building rafts using the types of tools that these peoples would have had, to recreate their general route and technology. We still know very little about this process and may never know more unless we are lucky enough to discover fragments of one of these ancient craft.

The peopling of places like Australia is an excellent example of the questions that archaeologists ask about ancient travel, questions that include why should people bother to move, how long have people been moving for, how did people move and what comprised the cognition and technology underlying their movement? At the most fundamental level are the questions that archaeologists ask about why people bother to move in relation to the *scale* of their movement. These questions come in terms of the numbers of people involved, the number of journeys made, whether the journeys were repeated or not, and the distances people travelled. This raises the issue of risk management: how dangerous these journeys were (or were perceived to be) and thus the cost benefit of such travel. It is clear, for example, that while many journeys in the past involved a greater risk of death than many people in the modern world would consider acceptable, this is not to suggest that people were careless with their own or others' lives in the past. Rather, there was clearly some calculation of risk and some attempts, whether adapting behaviour or developing technology, to reduce that risk. Archaeological evidence of ancient seafaring technologies, for example, shows the use of vessels well-suited to their environment, appropriate clothing and food, and often-ingenious navigational equipment. This technology meant that seafaring in the distant past was often no more dangerous than it would have been before the twentieth-century development of advanced safety and navigational devices.

Archaeological sites relating to human travel and transport are among some of the most dramatic that survive. They include shipwrecks, ports and harbours, roads and other transport infrastructure, some of which are in the most incredible of physical locations: stunning coastal shipwreck sites, bridges spanning deep gorges and roads ascending extraordinarily steep gradients. The archaeology of travel and transport also includes modern archaeological sites of the recent past. These include poignant locations, created in living memory, especially the wrecks of aircraft and vessels from the two world wars of the twentieth century. A new field of study is the archaeology of the Cold War, the study of the physical traces of the extraordinary period of technological innovation – much of it related to travel and transport, albeit with a military focus – of the 1950s to 1990s.

NEANDERTHAL VOYAGES IN THE AEGEAN

An intriguing new chapter in the story of prehistoric seafaring emerged in 2012. A team led by the archaeologist George Ferentinos, from the University of Patras, revealed new data that may necessitate a reconsideration of prehistoric global colonisation timelines and technologies. Ferentinos's team identified the first evidence for early seafaring in the southern Ionian Islands (Kefallinia and Zakynthos) some time between 110,000 and 35,000 years BP and possibly as far back as 200,000 years BP.

Archaeological data from the southern Ionian Islands show human habitation since the Middle Palaeolithic, dating back to 110,000 years BP. However, bathymetry (the study of lake or ocean floors), sea-level records and geological data all show that Kefallinia and Zakynthos were islands throughout this period, even if their land mass was larger and thus their distance from the mainland shorter. Consequently, human presence on the islands *must* have necessitated inter-island and island–mainland seafaring, seafaring that would, on the basis of prehistoric sea-level models, most likely have started some time between 110,000 and 35,000 years BP. These data push back the previous earliest date for the emergence of seafaring in the region, which has traditionally been placed at about 30,000 years BP on the basis of finds of Aurignacian (an upper Palaeolithic culture) stone tools in Sicily that must have been carried to the island by sea. Perhaps most fascinating of all, these new data indicate that these first seafarers were of the now extinct hominid species, the Neanderthals, who died out some time around 33–24,000 years BP. This species has not traditionally been associated with seafaring, which has been seen as the preserve of biologically modern humans.

While no actual vessels or other direct evidence of seafaring has been identified by the team, the presence of Neanderthals on the islands appears to have been encouraged by the coastal config- uration, which offered the right conditions for developing seafar- ing skills. The presence of Middle and Upper Palaeolithic sites in Kefallinia and Zakynthos suggests that these communities travelled to the islands from the Greek mainland using two routes. One route was from the southernmost extremity of the present-day island of Lefkada, which at that time was a peninsula; it involved two sea crossings, with approximately 5 and 7.5 km between intervening islets. The other route was from the Greek mainland and involved three crossings of between 5 and 12 km.

People have been travelling for long as there have *been* people, and even before, if the evidence for Neanderthal seafaring is true. However, relating to the issue of scale and risk, it is also clear that for a long time the scale (and so risk) of this travel was small and mainly involved relatively local movement in pursuit of resources.

We must emphasise that the global peopling of the world was by no means a planned activity. No Australian Indigenous ances- tor arrived on the continent in a meaningful act of exploration and colonisation, in the manner of more recent voyagers. People generally do things only when prompted by need or threat. In some cases, prehistoric travel was clearly motivated by the lure of resources; people following the migratory routes of the animals that they hunted, or moving down rivers in search of more space to live as their population grew. In others, travel was motivated by increased competition for or conflict over resources. But such a pragmatic approach to the evidence for ancient travel does not explain the case of the peopling of Australia, where there is no immediately obvious reason for making repeated open-water crossings. One aspect of the archaeology of travel is thus to consider the intangible motivations of humans to travel, which in some cases appears to come down to pure wanderlust; human beings' apparently innate impulse to explore.

Hunter-gatherer migrations

The earliest journeys were undoubtedly the local, repeated travels made in all sorts of places by our oldest ancestors. Many of these journeys will have been over relatively short distances and of limited duration, around a territory of resources: food and water to gather, animals to hunt and resources such as flint, clay and plants to collect. We know very little of these prehistoric journeys from archaeology. The most common traces are found not *en route* but at campsites, some clearly used by many generations over thousands of years. The campsites are rarely ever more than scatters of burning from fires, fragments of worked flint discarded from tool making and – if we are really lucky – the remains of animal bones from the hunt. Only the ethnographic study of the world's few remaining hunter-gatherer communities provides some insight into the social structures of such communities, including hierarchies on the basis of age or gender. This provides some small insight into what prehistoric journeys must have been like; modest in nature, undertaken by small groups of extended family, travelling very lightly across the landscape, carrying a few tools, and hunting and gathering food, fuel and other necessities as they went.

In terms of archaeology, what is most interesting is not precisely *how* such journeys were made but rather their long-term impact on the spread of humans around the world from about eighty thousand years ago. Clearly, as human populations grew, resources came under increasing pressure, a pressure that led to the gradual dispersal of people. The full reasons underlying this process, and its precise timings, are still not fully understood. In this sense, such colonisation was planned in that it was a response to a problem: the pressure of competition for limited resources. However, a colonisation movement given an impetus by the scarcity of resources should not be misunderstood as being planned in the sense that we in the modern world plan to go on holiday. Our prehistoric ancestors did not sit down around their campfire and decide that 'tomorrow we will move to new location "X"'. Rather, it was a long, drawn-out process, occurring over tens of thousands of years, undertaken by generations of people gradually moving into new areas. Not until around 70–50,000 years ago did our ancestors move out of Africa and into Asia; not until 40–30,000 years ago did the first colonists of North America move from Beringia; and not until thousands of years later did they move from the top of North America down the western coastline into Central, and eventually South, America.

Viking age exploration

Studies of Viking Age exploration offer a very different example of ancient journeying. Here, in comparison to prehistoric voyages, we are lucky enough to have a rich array of archaeological evidence, including remains of the types of boats used, evidence of the settlements, and a wonderful array of historical data, including the sagas, originally orally transmitted songs and stories that were later written down, and manuscript descriptions, illuminations and other artworks.

Viking voyages were made for very mixed reasons. The traditional view is one of hit-and-run raids on coastal settlements, something that clearly did take place in some cases. But other journeys were longer, taking months or even years, and subtler in intent and process, including trading and reconnaissance voyages to connect with new communities and potential trading contacts, formal colonisation voyages to set up new communities, which took with them hunting, farming and household equipment, and voyages of exploration born of pure curiosity and wanderlust.

In terms of the nature of these voyages, popular perception visualises hardy warriors in open-decked ships, braving the rigours of the unforgiving North Atlantic. While aspects of this are true, for Viking ships of all types were open-decked, and the people on board slept wrapped in oilskins, clothes and blankets, such a simple image belies the complexity of the situation. Archaeological discoveries across north-west Europe and Scandinavia have shown the Vikings to be excellent as well as cautious seafarers, with a keen eye for the weather and familiar with specialised navigational tools and techniques. Their voyages were normally made in the best possible conditions, in late spring, summer and early autumn, which offered more hours of daylight, fewer storms and warmer temperatures. Crucially, they also used a variety of types of vessel. Those used in long-distance open-water voyages were much larger, deeper and wider than the traditional Viking longship, offering better protection from the elements and more space for cargo. Such voyages often included a mix of people of different ages and sexes, and had a wide geographic spread. The North Sea and North Atlantic was one zone of operation but these people also travelled around the coasts of north-west Europe, across the Baltic Sea and in some cases far down into mainland central and east Europe, following the major estuarine rivers many thousands of miles inland. As outlined in the archaeologist Jan Bill's 2007 book, *The Sea Stallion from Glendalough: A Viking Longship Recreated*, experimental archaeology has shown the exceptional seagoing qualities of these vessels. Reconstructions of archaeological finds of such vessels have sailed the world – including the deep oceans – and they are capable of coping with a wide range of weather.

Thinking about travelling

A lot of attention among archaeologists is focused on the issue of landscape learning: how people developed and exploited their cognition as related to movement. Despite the benefits of modern navigational technologies such as maps and GPS, humans still exhibit this behaviour daily, in the regular journeys that we make from home to work, and to shops, school or social venue; the journeys that we just know the routes of and requirements for and do not have to think about.

Even on longer journeys, we still exhibit some of our ancient skills. We may glean evidence from our observation of the landscape, such as the location and height of the sun, the position of clouds, the movement of migratory birds or the presence of smoke on the horizon, as well as evidence of other humans and their journeys. The latter might include waymarks made from piles of stones (cairns), marks in the ground or large, visible activities on the horizon, the largest of which, in the modern world, are towns and cities.

Some of these journeying aids are bushcraft skills, of the type that are increasingly popular in the industrialised world, but others have largely been lost. How many modern people would be willing to make an extended open-water voyage in a boat with no modern navigational aids? And how many people could help build that vessel from scratch: find the timber, fell the

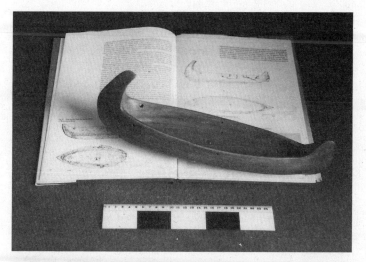

Figure 11 Replica of a thirteenth-century CE model boat found in the Viking city of Dublin (copyright and courtesy of Alisdair Roach)

trees, make the planks and nails, build the hull, make and lay the rigging and sails? People in the past had such skills and in most cases learnt them from early childhood, by observation of and participation in their family group.

An intriguing example of the evidence for ancient travel is the remnants of travel toys that archaeologists occasionally discover, from toy horses and carriages to boats. For example, numerous Viking Age boat models and ship graffiti – naive scratched outlines of vessels – hint at countless Viking children playing with and thinking about boats and the voyages that they might undertake.

Transport technologies

As soon as people developed the cognition of travel, it is clear that they began to develop the *technology* of travel. At its simplest,

Figure 12 Reconstruction of the use of the thirteenth-century CE model boat found in Dublin (copyright of Jane Brayne and Alisdair Roach and courtesy of Alisdair Roach)

people can, and still do, simply walk to and fro. But, depending on the environment (including the season), and our age and health, walking is a limited option, both in terms of the distance it is possible to travel and the load that we can carry. Shoes offer an immediate improvement, protecting the feet, as does making bags to carry objects in. But to travel further and faster, food, tools, clothing, overnight shelter and possibly goods to trade and exchange, are needed. Such increases in travelling sophistication and complexity require the development of specific travel technologies, even for relatively modest journeys.

Travel technologies require a host of resources and specialist skills that must be developed and refined over time. Some skills may be derived from everyday skills (for example, metal- or woodworking) but others may be more specialised, for example, boatbuilding. There are also related technologies, such as the domestication and breeding of animals like horses and cattle, which feed the development of tools such as bridles and stirrups. Other travel technologies meet the more popularly understood meaning of the term, for example, the development of wheeled vehicles, from the humble cart to the modern supercar by way of specialist technologies such as the bicycle.

In a chapter on the archaeology of travel it is useful to consider the peculiarities of transport technology, both in terms of what archaeological evidence survives and also what such technologies tell us of their broader social, cultural, environmental, mental and physical determinants. Maritime archaeology provides particularly useful examples, partly because of the good rates of survival of shipwrecks in comparison to many sites on land and also because, as the maritime archaeologist Keith Muckelroy (1951–1980) wrote in 1978: 'in any pre-industrial society, from the upper Palaeolithic to the nineteenth century AD, a boat or (later) a ship was the largest and most complex machine produced'.

A good example of Muckelroy's dictum regarding the complexity of past seafaring technology is the series of archaeological remains of what are termed 'sewn plank boats' that survives from Bronze Age Britain. Two sites in particular have provided a wealth of data about north-west European Bronze Age ship technology, which, when compared to one another provide archaeologists with a unique insight into these societies' technological abilities. These sites have also allowed us a better insight into wider Bronze Age society, including its trade relationships and social structures.

The first site is Ferriby, which lies on the north bank of the River Humber near the port city of Kingston upon Hull in north-east England. As discussed in Chapter 2, over the course of nearly thirty years, from 1931, a team of archaeologists uncovered the remains of three boats, the first and most complete vessel dating from about 1880–1680 BCE, the second from about 1940–1720 BCE and the third from about 2030–1780 BCE. The second site is Dover, a major port on the south-east coast of England. In 1992, a team of archaeologists working in advance of the building of a new road system discovered the remains of a similar type of vessel to those known from Ferriby, eventually dating the vessel to around 1575–1520 BCE. Compared to similar finds from elsewhere in Europe, vessels such as those from Ferriby and Dover demonstrate the shipbuilding technologies and techniques peculiar to these Bronze Age communities. Using no iron tools or fastenings (iron technology was some way off), they successfully and regularly felled large trees (often oaks) to create the long, wide planks that meant they could build vessels at least twelve metres long: the first Ferriby boat has an estimated length of thirteen metres; the Dover boat is approximately the same.

These vessels' planks were literally sewn together. Holes were drilled at regular intervals along their length and either strong withies (flexible pieces of wood, often willow or hazel) or ropes made of natural plant materials such as lime bast (the soft inner layer of the lime tree's bark) were pushed through the holes and intricately fastened together to form a watertight hull. Materials such as moss and grass, together with natural sealants like animal fat, were pushed between the planks to further enhance their watertightness. Once complete, it is clear that such vessels were capable of long voyages, although there is debate as to whether they carried sails or were paddled. In some cases their voyages were along the coastline but in other circumstances, such as at Dover, they probably undertook cross-channel voyages for trade and exchange. Such vessels were clearly central to their communities' lifestyle and identity, offering them access to imported materials and ideas. Building such craft also clearly represented a major commitment of communal time and resources.

A different example of archaeological evidence for specialised transport technologies came to light in 1962, on the banks of the River Weser near the city of Bremen, Germany. This discovery, the remains of a strangely shaped ship, transformed our understanding of medieval technology. Subsequent analyses proved that the vessel dated from around 1380 CE and that it was nearly complete when lost, possibly swept away in a winter storm. What was important about this discovery (which became known as the Bremen Cog) was that it verified previously unsubstantiated hypotheses about the type, and crucially the shape, of the cargo ships used in the area in this period primarily by the Hanseatic League, an alliance of medieval trading cities that operated across the North and Baltic Seas. A variety of different iconographic sources, particularly the wax seals used on official documents of this period but also images in illuminated manuscripts, had long been recognised as depicting a particular shape of vessel, referred to as a *cog* or *kogge*. However, it was hypothesised that these depictions were stylised, deliberately exaggerating certain details and playing others down, as the simple shape of the vessels, with a flat bottom, a steeply angled bow and stern, and a single central mast carrying a square sail, seemed unlikely.

The discovery of the Bremen cog was crucial in that it demonstrated, for the first time, that the depictions were realistic and cogs really were shaped in this unlikely way. More than twenty-four remains of other cogs have been discovered around the coasts of north-west Europe since that first one, refining our understanding of the origins and development of this unique type of vessel. The strange shape of the medieval cog turns out to be a design compromise among a series of cultural and environmental demands and determinants. There was the cultural demand to have a cheap, easily built and maintained, and above all capacious ship capable of undertaking regular voyages carrying large cargos of barrels of wine, bundles of metal or crates of pottery (all of which have been discovered on wrecked cogs). There were also the environmental determinants of the cogs' normal operating area, the shallow water and muddy, tidal coasts of the southern North Sea and Baltic, where vessels needed to be sturdy and able to sit upright in harbour when the tide went out, allowing them to be unloaded easily, without needing quays or wharfs. The cogs' odd shape represents the compromise necessary to meet these conflicting demands and determinants. This has been verified by experimental archaeology; full-scale replicas of the Bremen cog have been built and sailed. Overall, this type of vessel is an object lesson in the relationship between archaeological and documentary data in the understanding of cultural and environmental impetuses on transport technology.

A third and final useful example of archaeological evidence for specialised transport technologies is that found in perhaps the most unexpected locations of all: rivers such as the Mississippi, Missouri and Ohio in the USA. These rivers, and the vessels that travelled along them, were crucial in the opening of the West in nineteenth-century America, that great population movement and expansion beyond the older coastal zone settlements of the eastern seaboard. Before the later expansion of the railway network, paddle steamers were the only easy way to reach large sections of the central United States, but the technology of such vessels had to meet a series of conflicting cultural and environmental determinants. The relatively shallow but fast-flowing rivers where these vessels operated demanded they had a limited draught (below-water hull depth). These boats had to be reliable, following regular, scheduled routes along the rivers and between specific locations, which demanded consistent, although not

Figure 13 Archaeologists at work on the wreck of the steamboat *Montana*, near Bridgeton, Missouri (copyright of the PAST Foundation and the Maritime Studies Program, East Carolina University, courtesy of Annalies Corbin)

necessarily rapid, motive power. The vessels had to offer large cargo and passenger capacities while coping with the relative scarcity of refuelling depots (at least at first), so they had to be able to carry considerable amounts of fuel. The result was the coal- or sometimes wood-fired paddle steamer: long, low, shallow-hulled vessels, usually with a single large paddle wheel at the stern; vessels whose heyday was short.

Traces of some of the vessels survive in places along these rivers, especially along the Missouri, abandoned where they were last used, dumped or wrecked. The remains of several such vessels have been intensively analysed, for example that of the *Montana*, lost in 1884 on the Missouri River near Bridgeton, Missouri. In the winter of 2001–2002, unusually low water levels exposed the remains of the *Montana* for the first time since the mid 1960s, enabling a survey and excavation to take place. Such analyses give an insight into a design and technology that developed 'on the hoof', involved numerous shipyards and craftspeople, had little in the way of a formal design process, and was constantly modified by owners and operators. Archaeological studies also reveal aspects of the life of the passengers and crew of such vessels; these studies complement contemporary descriptions of journeys and evidence from other sources such as early photos.

7

The future of
archaeology

Hopefully, I have whetted your appetite for learning more about archaeology; perhaps even for getting involved in an archaeological project. How you can do that is outlined below but it is important to remember that the future of archaeology lies in all our hands, even if you never intend to get your hands dirty.

Around the world, the vast majority of archaeological fieldwork is undertaken on behalf of everyone, through different forms of government funding, both direct and indirect. A university archaeologist excavating a site in South America might ask a different series of questions about the past than a government archaeologist working in advance of a new road scheme in China or a commercial archaeologist working on the site of a new housing development in Australia, but they all get the majority of their funding, as well as their permission to work on sites, from the governments of their respective nations. Some funding comes directly from government in the form of grants and awards, while other funding comes indirectly, through laws and regulations that require businesses to pay for archaeological investigations in advance of developments such as new buildings, roads or energy transmission systems. The key point is that, as citizens, we all have a stake in archaeology because it belongs to all of us, now and in the future: to our children, grandchildren and great-grandchildren, protected and managed on our behalf by our governments. One of the futures of archaeology lies in the greater recognition of the shared global ownership of the past. And shared ownership brings with it the need for greater awareness of the awesome responsibility it entails.

Archaeologists increasingly work in partnerships across international borders, because modern borders and boundaries don't necessarily reflect ancient ones. Archaeologists also increasingly share more and more data online, under open access conditions. The Internet has been transformative in this respect, as it has been for many other branches of the arts and sciences. Archaeologists also work in nations that have less happy histories of exploration and discovery; for example, countries in Africa, such as Angola, which suffered grievously from war and famine in the past, something that precluded the study of their archaeological remains. Happily, many of these countries are now more stable, allowing archaeological exploration to occur, as well as, crucially, community involvement, education and training. Alas, for every country that becomes more stable and allows archaeological fieldwork to occur, another seems to fall into trouble. Syria, for example, has a long and proud history of archaeological fieldwork but, since its descent into civil war in 2011, fieldwork has stopped and, even worse, archaeological sites and museums have been looted, damaged and destroyed.

Sadly, catastrophes such as war and famine are not the only things that put the future of archaeology at risk. Global climate change, now almost universally recognised as both being caused by humans and a threat to all our lives, already affects the survival and integrity of archaeological sites, especially in low-lying areas such as the coasts of the Indian and Pacific oceans. This is a trend that the IPCC (the Intergovernmental Panel on Climate Change) and its cultural heritage partner UNESCO (the United Nations Educational, Scientific and Cultural Organization) expect only to become worse in the twenty-first century. These and other threats to archaeology are explored in more detail in a book I published with my colleague Marcy Rockman in 2012: *Archaeology in Society: Its Contemporary Relevance*.

More positively, new technologies are transforming archaeology. New remote-sensing and data-processing technologies allow us to learn more about the past by non-invasive means. Thanks to such survey technologies, whether satellite- or aeroplane-mounted, pulled along the ground or dropped into the deepest oceans, we learn more and more about our common past every day. And once the survey data have been collected, faster and faster data processing allows them to be more efficiently and effectively analysed.

The borders of archaeology are ever expanding: archaeologists are even starting to look into outer space. The Australian archaeologist Alice Gorman (aka 'Dr Spacejunk' on Twitter), is an internationally recognised leader in the emerging field of space archaeology, analysing, using archaeological methods and approaches, the debris of the 'space race' that started in the 1960s. The future of archaeology lies everywhere, and never have there been greater opportunities for all of us to be involved.

Getting involved

Getting involved in archaeology means a lot of different things. By reading this book, surfing archaeological websites or watching television programmes about archaeology, you are involved. You might become involved by attending talks about archaeology or taking a course. There are popular magazines about archaeology, notably *British Archaeology* and *Current Archaeology* in the UK and *Archaeology Magazine* in the USA, and similar publications in other countries. But in most people's mind's eye, involvement is likely to mean going on a dig and getting your hands dirty. And this is extremely easy to do.

Around the world, thousands of archaeological clubs and societies offer an opportunity to do 'real' archaeology: working on real sites, learning how to undertake real practical work and making a real contribution to our better understanding of the past. Such organisations have cheap (or even free) membership, are rarely more than a short journey from most people's homes and have members of different ages and experiences. There are national organisations, such as the Council for British Archaeology (CBA) in the UK, and specifically for those aged between 8 and 16, the CBA's Young Archaeologists Club (YAC); organisations equivalent to the YAC operate in the USA and other countries. Such clubs are the ideal way not only to become involved in archaeology but also to meet like-minded people. Involvement in the fieldwork of such organisations is often free, and if there is a charge it is usually kept very low, to cover costs rather than make a profit. The aim of such organisations is always the same: to encourage and facilitate public involvement in archaeology. Fieldwork organised by reputable archaeological charities will be well managed, safe and entertaining; participants will do a lot and learn a lot. For those interested in formally learning about archaeology there are many opportunities for study. Archaeology courses and classes are ideal for those who do not want, or are unable, to undertake practical fieldwork. These kinds of study can be done cheaply, fairly close to home and without major upheaval.

Formal university study is the next obvious step for budding archaeologists. However, university courses – whether full or part-time – can take many years, require a move to a different city or at least a regular commute, demand long hours of work and cost thousands of pounds in fees. But more than ninety-five percent of professional archaeologists have at least a Bachelor's (first) degree and many have a Master's degree or a

PhD. A degree in archaeology is the first step on the professional ladder of archaeology for those who think that they would like to pursue it as a career. My book *Becoming an Archaeologist: A Guide to Professional Pathways*, published in 2011, has more detail on voluntary and educational opportunities, as well as formal employment opportunities for archaeologists around the world.

Further reading

I hoped this book would draw you into the world of archaeological exploration; part of that process is the discovery of the countless publications that have been written about archaeological sites, approaches, tools and techniques over the years. These suggested further readings offer follow-up information on the sites and approaches discussed in this book but can only be a starting point for further exploration. It is worth mentioning that an excellent purchase for any archaeologist, no matter their experience, is a dictionary of archaeology that helps explains specific details. Timothy Darvill's 2008 *Concise Oxford Dictionary of Archaeology* is an excellent choice but other publishers produce similar dictionaries that can be purchased very cheaply. It is worth bearing in mind that more and more archaeological publications are available online as e-books, and also that even the most modest of local libraries is likely to stock at least a few core works of archaeology, so access to publications is very easy and need not incur much, if any, expense.

Chapter 1: Defining archaeology

Aston, M. 2006. *Interpreting the Landscape: Landscape, Archaeology and Local History*. New York: Taylor and Francis.

Barker, P. 1993. *Techniques of Archaeological Excavation*. London: Routledge.

Díaz-Andreu, M. and Champion, T. C. (eds.). 1996. *Nationalism and Archaeology in Europe*. London: UCL Press.

Fagan, B. M. 2004. *A Brief History of Archaeology: Classical Times to the Twenty-First Century*. New York: Pearson.

Fagan, G. G. (ed.). 2006. *Archaeological Fantasies: How Pseudoarchaeology Misrepresents the Past and Misleads the Public*. London: Routledge.

Holtorf, C. 2005. *From Stonehenge to Las Vegas: Archaeology as Popular Culture*. Walnut Creek: AltaMira.

Holtorf, C. 2007. *Archaeology is a Brand: the Meaning of Archaeology in Contemporary Popular Culture*. Walnut Creek: Left Coast Press.

King, T. F. 2004. *Cultural Resource Laws and Practice*. Walnut Creek: AltaMira.

Renfrew, C. 1999. *Before Civilization: the Radiocarbon Revolution and Prehistoric Europe*. London: Pimlico.

Renfrew, C. and Bahn, P. 2008. *Archaeology, Theories, Methods and Practice*. London: Thames and Hudson.

Roberts, A. 2009. *The Incredible Human Journey: the Story of How We Colonized the Planet*. London: BBCE Books.

Roberts, C. A. 2009. *Human Remains in Archaeology: A Handbook*. York: Council for British Archaeology.

Schapp, A. 1996. *Discovery of the Past: the Origins of Archaeology*. London: British Museum Press.

Chapter 2: Tools and techniques

Aitken, M. J. 1990. *Science-based Dating in Archaeology*. London: Longman.

Ballard, R. D. (ed.). 2008. *Archaeological Oceanography*. Princeton: Princeton University Press.

Barker, P. 1993. *Techniques of Archaeological Excavation*. London: Routledge.

Bowden, M. 1999. *Unravelling the Landscape: Inquisitive Approach to Archaeology*. London: Routledge.

Carver, M. 2009. *Archaeological Investigation*. London: Routledge.

Collins, J. M. and Molyneaux, B. 2003. *Archaeological Survey*. Walnut Creek: AltaMira.

Deetz, J. 1996. *In Small Things Forgotten: An Archaeology of Early American Life, revised edition*. New York: Doubleday.

Fulford, M. 2002. *A Guide to Silchester: The Roman Town of Calleva Atrebatum*. Reading: Calleva Trust.

Gater, J. and Gaffney, C. F. 2003. *Revealing the Buried Past: Geophysics for Archaeologists*. London: The History Press.

Green, J. 2004. *Maritime Archaeology: A Technical Handbook*. London: Academic Press.

Howard, P. 2006. *Archaeological Surveying and Mapping: Recording and Depicting the Landscape*. London: Routledge.

Johnson, M. 2010. *Archaeological Theory: An Introduction*. Oxford: Blackwell.

Little, B. J. 1992. *Text-aided Archaeology*. Boca Raton: CRC Press.

Malainey, M. E. 2010. *A Consumer's Guide to Archaeological Science*. New York: Springer.

O'Connor, T. and Evans, G. J. 2005. *Environmental Archaeology: Principles and Methods*. London: The History Press.

Orton, C. 2000. *Sampling in Archaeology*. New York: Cambridge University Press.

Rathje, W. L. and Murphy, C. 1992. *Rubbish! The Archaeology of Garbage*. New York: HarperCollins.

Robinson, W. S. 1998. *First Aid for Underwater Finds*. Portsmouth: Nautical Archaeology Society.

Schofield, J. 2011. *London 1100–1600: the Archaeology of a Capital City*. London: Equinox.

Sullivan, L. P. and Childs, S. T. 2003. *Curating Archaeological Collections: From the Field to the Repository*. Walnut Creek: AltaMira.

Stutz, L. N. 2003. *Embodied Rituals and Ritualized Bodies: Tracing Ritual Practices in Late Mesolithic Burials*. Stockholm: Almquiest and Wiksell.

Thompson, K. and Carter, P. 2005. *Sources for Local Historians*. London: Phillimore.

Watkinson, D. and Neal, V. 1998. *First Aid for Finds*. Hertford: RESCUE: The British Archaeological Trust.

Wilson, D. R. 2000. *Air Photo Interpretation for Archaeologists*. London: The History Press.

Wiseman, J. and El-Baz, F. (eds.). 2007. *Remote Sensing in Archaeology*. New York: Springer.

Wright, E. 1994. *North Ferriby and the Bronze Age Boats*. Hull: Ferriby Heritage Group.

Zimmerman, L. J. 2003. *Presenting the Past*. Walnut Creek: AltaMira.

Chapter 3: The archaeology of objects

Baxter, J. E. 2005. *The Archaeology of Childhood: Children, Gender and Material Culture*. Walnut Creek: AltaMira.

Bowden, M. 1999. *Unravelling the Landscape: Inquisitive Approach to Archaeology*. London: Routledge.

Freeman, C. and Louçã, F. 2002. *As Time Goes By: From the Industrial Revolution to the Information Revolution*. Oxford: Oxford University Press.

Gardiner, J. 2005. *Before the Mast: Life and Death Aboard the Mary Rose*. Portsmouth: Mary Rose Trust.

Hume, I. N. 1974. *All the Best Rubbish: the Classic Ode to Collecting*. New York: HarperCollins.

Hurcombe, L. M. 2007. *Archaeological Artefacts as Material Culture*. London: Routledge.

Marsden, P. 2003. *Sealed by Time: The Loss and Recovery of the Mary Rose*. Portsmouth: Mary Rose Trust.

Standage, T. A. 2007. *A History of the World in Six Glasses*. New York: Atlantic Books.

Stroulia, A. 2010. *Flexible Stones: Ground Stone Tools from Franchthi Cave*. Bloomington: Indiana University Press.

Taylor, T. 2010. *The Artificial Ape: How Technology Changed the Course of Human Evolution*. New York: Palgrave Macmillan.

Chapter 4: The archaeology of places

Alfrey, J. and Clark, C. 1993. *The Landscape of Industry: Patterns of Change in the Ironbridge Gorge*. London: Routledge.

Ashenburg, K. 2009. *Clean: An Unsanitised History of Washing*. London: Profile.

Aston, M. 2009. *Monasteries in the Landscape*. London: Amberley.

Barker, G. 2006. *The Agricultural Revolution in Prehistory: Why Did Foragers Become Farmers?* Oxford: Oxford University Press.

Baxter, J. E. 2005. *The Archaeology of Childhood: Children, Gender and Material Culture*. Walnut Creek: AltaMira.

Bell, M. 2013. *The Bronze Age in the Severn Estuary*. York: Council for British Archaeology Research Report 172.

Bond, J. 2004. *Monastic Landscapes*. Stroud: Tempus.

Bowsher, J. 2012. *Shakespeare's London Theatreland: Archaeology, History and Drama*. London: Museum of London Archaeology.

Breeze, D. J. and Dobson, B. 2000. *Hadrian's Wall*. London: Penguin.

Brodie, A., Croom, J. and Davies, J. O. 1999. *Behind Bars: the Hidden Architecture of England's Prisons*. London: English Heritage.

Casella, E. C. 2007. *The Archaeology of Institutional Confinement*. Gainesville: University Press of Florida.

Cantwell, A-M. E. and di Zerega Wall, D. 2001. *Unearthing Gotham: the Archaeology of New York City*. New Haven: Yale University Press.

Cowan, C., Seeley, F., Wardle, A., Westman, A. and Wheeler, L. (eds.). 2008. *Roman Southwark – Settlement and Economy: Excavations in Southwark 1973–1991*. London: Museum of London Archaeology Service.

Delgado, J. 2009. *Gold Rush Port: The Maritime Archaeology of San Francisco's Waterfront*. Los Angeles: University of California Press.

Edwards, D. 2005. 'The Archaeology of Religion', in M. Diaz-Andreu and S. Lucy (eds.). *The Archaeology of Identity*. London: Routledge.

Fishman, R. 1989. *Bourgeois Utopias: The Rise and Fall of Suburbia*. New York: Basic Books.

Gilchrist, R. 1997. *Gender and Material Culture: the Archaeology of Religious Women*. London: Routledge.

Harding, D. W. 2009. *The Iron Age Round-House: Later Prehistoric Building in Britain and Beyond*. Oxford: Oxford University Press.

Herrmann, G. 1997. *Early and Medieval Merv: a Tale of Three Cities*. London: British Academy.

Karskens, G. 1999. *Inside the Rocks: the Archaeology of a Neighbourhood*. Sydney: Hale and Iremonger.

Kyle, D. G. 2006. *Sport and Spectacle in the Ancient World*. New York: Wiley-Blackwell.

Mainstone, R. J. 1997. *Hagia Sophia: Architecture, Structure and Liturgy of Justinian's Great Church*. London: Thames and Hudson.

McAtackney, L. 2005. 'Long Kesh / Maze Prison: An Archaeological Opportunity', *British Archaeology* 84 (September/October): 10–15.

Morriss, R. K. 2004. *Roads: Archaeology and Architecture*. London: The History Press.

Rippon, S. 1997. *The Severn Estuary: Landscape Evolution and Wetland Reclamation*. Leicester: Leicester University Press.

Stern, R. M. 2013. *Paradise Planned: The Garden Suburb and the Modern City*. New York: Monacelli Press.

Tarlow, S. 2012. *The Archaeology of Improvement in Britain, 1750–1850*. Cambridge: Cambridge University Press.

Yegül, F. 2009. *Bathing in the Roman World*. Cambridge: Cambridge University Press.

Chapter 5: The archaeology of landscapes

Barnes, G. and Williamson, T. 2006. *Hedgerow History: Ecology, History and Landscape Character*. Stroud: Windgatherer Press.

Benjamin, J., Bonsall, C., Pickard, C. and Fischer, A. (eds.). 2011. *Submerged Prehistory*. Oxford: Oxbow.

Bradley, N. 2000. *An Archaeology of Natural Places*. London: Routledge.

Bradley, R. 1997. *Rock Art and the Prehistory of Atlantic Europe: Signing the Land*. New York: Routledge.

Burroughs, W. J. 2005. *Climate Change in Prehistory: the End of the Reign of Chaos*. Cambridge: Cambridge University Press.

Chapman, H. 2006. *Landscape Archaeology and GIS*. London: The History Press.

Coles, B. 1998. 'Doggerland: a Speculative Survey', *Proceedings of the Prehistoric Society* 64: 45–81.

Conolly, J. and Lake, M. 2006. *Geographical Information Systems in Archaeology*. Cambridge: Cambridge University Press.

Delgado, J. 2009. *Nuclear Dawn: The Atomic Bomb, from the Manhattan Project to the Cold War*. New York: Osprey.

Evans, A., Flatman, J. and Flemming, N. 2014. *Prehistoric Archaeology on the Continental Shelf.* New York: Springer.

Fagan, B. G. 2000. *The Little Ice Age: How Climate Made History, 1300–1850*. New York: Basic Books.

Flood, J. 2000. *Archaeology of the Dreamtime: the Story of Prehistoric Australia and its People, revised edition*. Sydney: Angus and Robertson.

Gaffney, V., Fitch, S. and Smith, D. 2009. *Europe's Lost World: the Rediscovery of Doggerland*. York: Council for British Archaeology Research Report 160.

Hamilton, D. L. 2006. 'Pirates and Merchants: Port Royal, Jamaica', in R. K. Skowronek and C. R. Ewen (eds.). *X Marks the Spot: The Archaeology of Piracy*. Gainesville: University Press of Florida. 13–30.

Johnson, M. 2007. *Ideas of Landscape: An Introduction*. Oxford: Wiley-Blackwell.

Jones, M. 2001. *The Molecule Hunt: Archaeology and the Hunt for Ancient DNA*. London: Allen Lane.

Little, B. J. 1992. *Text-aided Archaeology*. Boca Raton: CRC Press.

Reid, C. 1913. *Submerged Forests*. Cambridge: Cambridge University Press.

Chapter 6: The archaeology of travelling

Bass, G. F. (ed.). 2005. *Beneath the Seven Seas: Adventures with the Institute of Nautical Archaeology*. London: Thames and Hudson.

Bill, J. 2007. *The Sea Stallion from Glendalough: A Viking Longship Recreated*. Roskilde: Viking Ship Museum.

Buchli, V. and Lucas, G. 2001. *Archaeologies of the Contemporary Past*. London: Routledge.

Corbin, A., Bradley, A. R, Bradford, J. R. and Smith, G. A. 2008. *The Steamboat 'Montana' and the Opening of the West*. Gainesville: University Press of Florida.

Crumlin-Pedersen, O. 2010. *Archaeology and the Sea in Scandinavia and Britain*. Roskilde: Viking Ship Museum.

Dixon, E. J. 1999. *Bones, Boats and Bison: Archaeology and the First Colonization of Western North America*. Albuquerque: University of New Mexico Press.

Englert, A. and Trakadas, A. (eds.). 2009. *Wulfstan's Voyage: The Baltic Sea Region in the Early Viking Age as Seen from Shipboard*. Roskilde: Viking Ship Museum.

Gardiner, R. (ed.). 1994. *Cogs, Caravels and Galleons: The Sailing Ship, 1000–1650*. London: Conway.

Gould, R. A. 2000. *Archaeology and the Social History of Ships*. Cambridge: Cambridge University Press.

Morritt, R. D. 2011. *Beringia: Archaic Migrations into North America*. Cambridge: Cambridge Scholars.

Skowronek, R. K. and Ewen, C. R. (eds.). 2006. *X Marks the Spot: The Archaeology of Piracy*. Gainesville: University Press of Florida.

Chapter 7: The future of archaeology

Flatman, J. 2011. *Becoming an Archaeologist: A Guide to Professional Pathways*. Cambridge: Cambridge University Press.

Nicolas, G. 2011. *Being and Becoming Indigenous Archaeologists*. Walnut Creek: Left Coast Press.

Rockman, M. and Flatman, J. (eds.). 2012. *Archaeology in Society: Its Contemporary Relevance*. New York: Springer.

Sabloff, J. 2008. *Archaeology Matters: Action Archaeology in the Modern World*. Walnut Creek: Left Coast Press.

Websites

Advisory Council on Underwater Archaeology: http://www.acuaonline.org/

The ACUA is the leading international organisation for maritime and underwater archaeology. If you want to learn more about this type of archaeology, start here.

The Archaeology Channel: http://www.archaeologychannel.org/

Home to a wealth of archaeology-related videos and podcasts, the Archaeology Channel is the archaeological community's YouTube and Spotify rolled into one.

Archaeology Data Service: http://archaeologydataservice.ac.uk/

The ADS supports research, learning and teaching with freely available, high-quality and dependable digital resources in archaeology.

Archaeological Institute of America: http://www.archaeological.org/

Publisher of *Archaeology* magazine, one of the leading popular magazines on archaeology, the AIA organises events around the world, including for younger members aged 21–45.

Australian Archaeological Association: http://www.australianar-chaeologicalassociation.com.au/

The AAA is the largest archaeological organisation in Australia, representing professionals, students and others. It publishes the highly respected *Australian Archaeology* journal.

British Archaeological Jobs and Resources: http://www.bajr.org/

For those professionals seeking work in archaeology in the UK, this is the place to look. BAJR provides useful guidance for students and volunteers on how to become involved in archaeology.

Cadw: http://cadw.wales.gov.uk/

Cadw is the Welsh Government's historic environment service.

Council for British Archaeology: http://new.archaeologyuk.org/

The CBA is the leading organisation for archaeology in the UK, acting as an umbrella organisation for amateurs and professionals. It publishes the popular magazine *British Archaeology*. The CBA is the parent organisation of the Young Archaeologists Club (YAC).

Current Archaeology: http://www.archaeology.co.uk/

Current Archaeology and its international version, *Current World Archaeology,* provide a regular stimulating tour around the best of the latest developments in archaeology.

tDAR (the Digital Archaeological Record): http://www.tdar.org/

tDAR is the digital repository of Digital Antiquity, a collaborative organisation dedicated to enhancing preservation and access to the digital records of archaeological investigations.

DigVentures: http://digventures.com/

DigVentures is a social business committed to raising seed capital for and increasing participation in sustainable archaeology and heritage projects worldwide.

Historic England: http://historicengland.org.uk

Historic England is the UK Government's historic environment service for sites in England.

European Association of Archaeologists: http://e-a-a.org/

The EAA is the association for professional archaeologists in Europe and beyond. Its eleven thousand members from sixty countries worldwide work in prehistoric, classical, medieval and later archaeology.

Heritage Gateway: http://www.heritagegateway.org.uk/gateway/

A website that allows you to cross-search over sixty resources on local and national heritage in England.

Historic Scotland: http://www.historic-scotland.gov.uk/

Historic Scotland is the Scottish Government's historic environment service.

Internet Archaeology: http://intarch.ac.uk/index.html

Internet Archaeology is the premier e-journal for archaeology, an open-access, independent, not-for-profit archaeological journal.

Institute for Archaeologists: http://www.archaeologists.net/

The Institute for Archaeologists (IfA) advances the practice of archaeology and allied disciplines by promoting professional standards and ethics for conserving, managing, understanding and promoting enjoyment of heritage.

National Parks Service archaeology programme: http://www. nps.gov/archeology/

The NPS provides a wealth of information on archaeology in the US National Parks, as well as explaining the legal requirements for undertaking archaeological investigation on Federal land.

Nautical Archaeology Society: http://www.nasportsmouth.org. uk/

The NAS is the oldest charity dedicated to the protection and promotion of maritime and underwater archaeology. Its training scheme is accredited around the world; once trained with the NAS you can volunteer on underwater projects in dozens of different countries.

OASIS (Online Access to the Index of Archaeological Investigations): http://oasis.ac.uk/pages/wiki/Main

OASIS is an online index to archaeological grey literature in the UK that has been produced as a result of the advent of large-scale, developer-funded fieldwork and a similar increase in fieldwork undertaken by volunteers.

Past Horizons: http://www.pasthorizonspr.com/

A popular online magazine covering archaeology and heritage news.

Portable Antiquities Scheme: http://www.finds.org.uk/

A UK-government-sponsored scheme, the PAS records amateur discoveries of small finds of all types. It has a network of regional advisers who can help identify, date and catalogue anything that you find, adding to the national understanding of the spread of different portable materials.

Register of Professional Archaeologists: http://rpanet.org/

The Register of Professional Archaeologists is a listing of archaeologists who have agreed to abide by an explicit code of conduct and standards of research performance.

RESCUE: the British Archaeological Trust: http://www.rescue-archaeology.org.uk/

RESCUE is a charity dedicated to lobbying for improved standards in, and the protection of, archaeological sites. Its newsletter, *Rescue News,* contains details of all its latest activities.

Society for American Archaeology: http://www.saa.org/

The SAA is an international organisation dedicated to the research, interpretation and protection of the archaeological heritage of the Americas. It publishes widely and offers training for volunteers.

Society for Historical Archaeology: http://www.sha.org/

A sister organisation of the SAA, the SHA focuses on the historical archaeology of the modern world (from approximately the sixteenth century to the present day), mainly in the Americas but also around the world. It publishes widely and offers training.

Shovelbums: http://www.shovelbums.org/

The American equivalent of the BAJR, Shovelbums is the place where everyone looks for jobs in archaeology in the USA. It provides useful guidance for students and volunteers on how to get involved in archaeology.

TrowelBlazers: http://trowelblazers.com/

TrowelBlazers is a celebration of women archaeologists, palaeontologists and geologists.

UNESCO: http://www.unesco.org/

UNESCO, the United Nations Educational, Scientific and Cultural Organization, provides a wealth of information about global cultural heritage, including archaeology.

World Archaeological Congress: http://www.worldarchaeologicalcongress.org/

The WAC is a non-governmental, not-for-profit organisation and is the only worldwide body representing practising archaeologists. The WAC seeks to promote interest in the past in all countries and is particularly useful for contacts in archaeology in the industrialising world.

Young Archaeologists Club: http://www.yac-uk.org/

The YAC is the only UK-wide club for young people up to the age of 17 who are interested in archaeology. The YAC's vision is for all young people to have opportunities to be inspired and excited by archaeology and to empower them to help shape its future.

Acknowledgements

I would like to thank first and foremost Rachel Beaumont, Paul Boone, Andrea D'Cruz, Marsha Filion, Mike Harpley, Juliet Mabey, Laura McFarlane and Fiona Slater at Oneworld for inviting me to write this book and then seeing it through to production; also Ann Grand for her crucial editorial work. Their advice and patience is greatly appreciated. Similarly, a number of anonymous peer reviewers made extremely useful suggestions on earlier drafts of this book and I thank them for their time and observations.

Colleagues too numerous to mention, at a series of employers, have been of considerable support in the writing of this book, in particular Roger Bowdler at Historic England, Patricia Reynolds at Surrey County Council and Stephen Shennan at University College London.

Thanks are particularly owed to the following individuals and organisations for kindly and most generously allowing me to reproduce photos to which they hold the copyright, including: Archaeology South-East, Martin Bell, Paul Belford, Jane Brayne, Mary Casey, Annalies Corbin, Sarah Dhanjal, the Maritime Studies Programme, East Carolina University, Historic England, Charlotte Frearson, Martin Gibbs, Courtney Nimura, the PAST Foundation, Dominic Perring and Alisdair Roach.

Most importantly of all I wish to thank my wife, Jennifer Young, for her endless love, support, patience and wisdom. This book is a much better one thanks to her contributions and, as she and my daughter Zoe have taught me, the key is a question of control.

Index

Archaeology / Archaeological
Archives   1, 9, 24, 26, 57–58,
    78
Artefact biographies   70–71, 89
And climate   75, 80, 120,
    132–33, 138–40, 142–46,
    164–65
Conservation of objects
    in   76–78
Dating in   5, 11, 16, 17, 27–37,
    65
    Absolute dating   28, 33–36,
        65
    Chronology   11, 27–37
    Radiocarbon dating   17, 28,
        33–36
    Relative dating   28–32, 65
    Seriation 12
    Stratigraphy   5, 27–32, 54
    Typology   16, 32–33
Definition of   1, 3, 4–5, 11, 22
Desk-based analyses of   24–26
And DNA   36–37
Ethics of   5–7, 9
Excavation   29–32, 49–55
And the First World War   12,
    63, 149
History of   3, 10–21, 79–81

And human remains   5–7, 54,
    95–96
Indigenous communities
    relationship to   6–7,
    16–19, 63, 91, 129, 130–31,
    150–51
    Ancestral materials of   7
    Australian   7, 91, 130–31,
        150–51
    And European
        colonisation   7, 17,
        130–31
    Human remains of   7
    Native American   7
    NAGPRA   7
And intangible cultural
    heritage   130–31
Laws about   7, 9, 12, 15–17,
    19–20
Logistics of   24, 37–38, 41,
    51–52
And museums   9, 41, 57, 85–86
Nazi involvement in   14–15
Organisations
    Advisory Council on
        Underwater Archaeology
        (ACUA)   176
    Ahnenerbe   15

Archaeological Data Service
     (ADS)   176
Archaeological Institute of
     America (AIA)   176
Australian Archaeological
     Association (AAA)   177
Cadw   177
Council for British
     Archaeology   19, 166,
     177
DigVentures   177
European Association
     of Archaeologists
     (EAA)   178
Historic England   178
Historic Scotland   178
Institute for Archaeologists
     (IFA)   178
US National Parks Service
     (NPS)   134–35, 178
Nautical Archaeology Society
     (NAS)   178
Parks Canada   138–39
Rescue: the British Trust for
     Archaeology   16, 179
Register of Professional
     Archaeologists
     (RPA)   179
Society for American
     Archaeology
     (SAA)   179
Scottish Coastal
     Archaeology and the
     Problem of Erosion
     (SCAPE)   143–44

Society for Historical
     Archaeology
     (SHA)   179
Society of Antiquaries of
     London   10
Trowelblazers   180
United National Educational,
     Scientific and
     Cultural Organisation
     (UNESCO)   112, 131,
     164–65, 180
World Archaeological
     Congress (WAC)   19,
     180
Young Archaeologists Club
     (YAC)   19, 166, 180
Periods
Anglo-Saxon   14–15, 122
Bronze Age   11, 35, 44,
     68–69, 136, 143, 157–59
Iron Age   11, 44, 94, 109–
     10, 136–37, 143, 144
Medieval   30–32, 63, 82,
     83, 86–87, 95–96, 99,
     101–02, 119, 122–23,
     125–26, 137, 139,
     159–60
Mesolithic   16, 59–60, 97–99
Neolithic   13, 18, 60
Palaeolithic   68, 149–50
Roman   15, 29, 33, 99,
     100–02, 123–25, 136
Stone Age   11
Viking   14–15, 85–86,
     138–39, 152–56

Popular perceptions of 1–2,
7–9, 14–15, 18–19, 20, 22,
49–50, 145–46
Post-excavation analyses
of 55–58, 77–78
Preservation of 5, 9, 12,
15–16, 17
Pseudo-archaeology 8
Public engagement in 5, 9,
18–19, 41, 57–58, 143–44
Remote sensing in 45–49,
121–22, 132, 165
Scale and sampling in 26–27,
38–39, 42–49, 95, 128–30
Science in 3–4, 9, 10–11,
17, 28, 32, 33–37, 56–57,
75–76, 95–96, 112–13, 164
And the Second World
War 14–15, 16, 32, 82,
149
Survey in 43–49, 53–54
Themes in
Environmental 4, 16,
26–27, 42, 44, 53, 71,
74–76, 79–81, 86, 95,
97–99, 105, 127–31,
133–34, 135–40,
142–46, 164–65
Experimental 66, 85–86,
148, 154, 160
Industrial 112–13
Maritime 85–87, 105,
155–62
Prehistoric 11, 13, 15, 17,
35–36, 48, 63, 65–66,
68–69, 75, 94, 95,
97–99, 109, 121, 136–37,
140–42, 144–45, 147–
49, 147–51, 151–52,
157–59
Rescue 16, 19
Underwater 16, 48–49,
135–35, 140–42,
145–46
Tools and techniques
of 22–61
And treasure hunting 3,
8–9, 17

Archaeological sites
In Africa 7, 12, 21, 36–37,
47, 70–71, 75, 108, 123,
147–48, 152, 164
In Egypt 12, 47, 70–71, 75,
123
In Asia 8, 14, 15, 19, 21, 35,
37, 40, 47, 69, 102–04, 106,
108–09, 144–45, 152, 163
In Afghanistan 8, 104
In China 21, 103, 163
In India 21
In Russia 47, 106, 144–45
In Tibet 15
In Turkmenistan 102–04
Merv 102–04
In Australia 7, 13, 16, 35–36,
45, 63, 90–92, 107, 108,
130–31, 147–49, 150–51,
163
Lake Mungo 148

Sydney 90–92
In Central America 21, 37,
    102, 103, 116–17, 145–46,
    152
Port Royal, Jamaica 145–46
In North America 7, 10, 16,
    39–40, 45, 48–49, 75, 79,
    90, 103, 107, 108, 118,
    138–39, 144–45, 160–62,
    165–66
  In Canada 138–39
  In the USA 7, 10, 16,
      39–40, 45, 48–49, 75,
      79, 90, 103, 107, 108,
      118, 144–45, 160–62,
      165–66
    Little Salt Spring,
        Florida 75
    Montana, Missouri
        160–62
    Outer Banks, North
        Carolina 48–49
    Tucson, Arizona 39–40
In South America 21, 37, 75,
    102, 116–17, 145, 152, 163
In Europe 10, 11, 13, 15–16,
    30–31, 34, 43–44, 45, 48,
    49, 52, 68–69, 74, 76–78,
    80–81, 94, 95–96, 97–99,
    100–02, 103, 108–09, 111,
    112–13, 115, 116, 119–21,
    122–26, 133–34, 141–42,
    143–44, 148, 149–50,
    155–56, 157–59, 159–60,
    165–67

Doggerland, North
    Sea 141–42
In Germany 15, 159–60
Bremen 159–60
In Greece 13, 15, 43–44,
    49, 68–69, 115, 123,
    149–50
  Kythera 43–44
  Melos 68–69
In Ireland 155–56
  Dublin 155–56
In Italy 13, 15, 80–81, 94,
    116, 123
Otzi, Austria / Italy 80–81
In Poland 15
In Turkey 15, 16, 18, 68–69,
    102, 115, 148
  Catalhoyuk 18, 102
  Haggia Sophia 115
  Uluburun 68–69, 148
In the UK 10, 11, 15–16,
    30–31, 34, 45, 48, 52, 74,
    76–78, 95–96, 97–99,
    100–02, 103, 108–09,
    111, 112–13, 119–21,
    122–26, 133–34, 143–
    44, 157–59, 165–67
  Baile Sear, Outer
      Hebrides 144
  Brisley Farm, Kent 34
  Chichester, Sussex 52
  Cruester, Isle of Bressay,
      Shetland 143
  Ferriby, Yorkshire 35,
      157–59

Fountains Abbey,
Yorkshire   95–96
Dover, Kent   157–59
Hadrian's Wall,
Northumbria
123–25
Ironbridge,
Shropshire   112–13
Kenilworth Castle,
Warwickshire   125–26
London   30–31, 100–02,
103, 121
Mary Rose,
Portsmouth   76–77
Sandwick, Isle of Unst,
Shetland   143
Scapa Flow, Orkney
Islands   48
Severn Estuary   97–99
Stonehenge,
Wiltshire   121–22
Sutton Hoo, Suffolk   74
In the Middle East   13, 15,
102–04, 164
In Iraq   13, 15
Jericho   13
In Syria   15, 164
In the Pacific   47, 134–35,
144–45, 147–48, 152
Beringia   144–45, 147–48,
152
Bikini Atoll, Marshall
Islands   134–35
Easter Island (Rapa Nui)   47

In Scandinavia   14, 15, 59–60,
60–61, 85–86, 136–37, 153
In Denmark   60–61, 85–86,
136
Hjortspring   136
Skuldelev   85–86
In Finland   15
In Norway   136–37
Hornes Mellom   136
In Sweden   15, 59–60
Skateholm   59–60

Archaeologists
Bass, George   16, 68–69
Bednarik, Robert   148
Bell, Martin   99
Bill, Jan   154
Bradley, Richard   137
Carver, Martin   23
Casella, Eleanor   107
Childe, Vere Gordon   13
Clarke, Grahame   16
Coles, Bryony   141–42
Deetz, James   40
Fahlander, Fredrik   60–61
Ferentinos, George   149–50
Flinders Petrie, William   12
Gorman, Alice   165
Hamilton, Donny   145–46
Harris, Edward   29
Harrison–Buck, Eleanor
116–17
Hodder, Ian   18, 88
Jacobsen, Thomas   68
Jefferson, Thomas   10

Johnson, Matthew 58, 125–26
Kenyon, Kathleen 13
Kidder, Alfred 13
Lane–Fox Pitt Rivers,
    Augustus 12
Mallowan, Max 14
McAtackney, Laura 107
Muckelroy, Keith 157
Parcak, Sarah 47
Piquette, Kathryn 70–71

Rathje, William 39
Rathz, Philip 16
Renfrew, Colin 17
Reynolds, Andrew 122
Rockman, Marcy 165
Stutz, Liv Nilsson 60–61
Tilley, Chris 18
Ucko, Peter 19
Wheeler, Mortimer 2, 13, 23
Wheeler, Tessa Verney 13